ANNE WILLAN'S
LOOK&COOK

Fruit Desserts

ANNE WILLAN'S
LOOK & COOK

Fruit Desserts

DORLING KINDERSLEY, INC.
NEW YORK

A DORLING KINDERSLEY BOOK

Created and Produced by
CARROLL & BROWN LIMITED
5 Lonsdale Road
London NW6 6RA

Editorial Director Jeni Wright
Editors Norma MacMillan
Stella Vayne
Sally Poole
Assisted by Joanna Pitchfork
Art Editor Vicky Zentner
Designers Lyndel Donaldson
Wendy Rogers
Lucy De Rosa
Mary Staples
Lisa Webb

First American Edition, 1992
10 9 8 7 6 5 4 3 2 1

Published in the United States by
Dorling Kindersley, Inc., 232 Madison Avenue
New York, New York 10016

Willan, Anne.
    Fruit desserts / by Anne Willan. – 1st American ed.
    p.   cm. – (Look and cook)
Includes index.
ISBN 1-56458-097-0
    1. Desserts   2. Cookery (Fruit)   I. Title.   II. Series: Willan,
Anne. Look and cook.
TX773.W67   1992
641.8'6 – dc20   92-4481
                                                        CIP

Reproduced by Colourscan, Singapore
Printed and bound in Italy by A. Mondadori, Verona

CONTENTS

FRUIT

THE LOOK & COOK APPROACH

Welcome to **Fruit Desserts** and the *Look & Cook* series. These volumes are designed to be the simplest, most informative cookbooks you'll ever own. They are the closest I can come to sharing my techniques for cooking my own favorite recipes without actually being with you in the kitchen looking over your shoulder.

Equipment and ingredients often determine whether or not you can cook a particular dish, so *Look & Cook* illustrates everything you need at the beginning of each recipe. You'll see at a glance how long a recipe takes to cook, how many servings it makes, what the finished dish looks like, and how much preparation can be done ahead. When you start to cook, you'll find the preparation and cooking are organized into easy-to-follow steps. Each stage is color-coded and everything is shown in photographs with brief text to go with each step. You will never be in doubt about what it is you are doing, why you are doing it, or how it should look.

EQUIPMENT

INGREDIENTS

🍽 SERVES 6   🥣 WORK TIME 30-35 MINUTES   🍲 COOKING TIME 25-35 MINUTES

I've also included helpful hints and ideas under "Anne Says." These may list an alternative ingredient or piece of equipment, or sometimes the reason for using a certain method is explained, or there is advice on mastering a particular technique. Similarly, if there is a crucial stage in a recipe when things can go wrong, I've included some warnings called "Take Care."

Many of the photographs are annotated to pinpoint why certain pieces of equipment work best, or how the food should look at that stage of cooking. Because presentation is so important, a picture of the finished dish and serving suggestions are at the end of each recipe.

Thanks to all this information, you can't go wrong. I'll be with you every step of the way. So please, come with me into the kitchen to look, cook, and create some exciting **Fruit Desserts.**

WHY FRUIT?

There is nothing better than a piece of fresh, sun-ripened fruit – except, of course, a luscious dessert made from it. The vibrant colors of berries, cherries, peaches, plums, among others are lovely to look at – and even better to eat! Whether in a simple salad, or a festive flambé, whether served hot or chilled, fruit is the basis for an unlimited range of dinner finales.

RECIPE CHOICE

Everyone has a favorite fruit dessert, whether it's Grandma's peach pie or all-American strawberry shortcake, or the French tarte Tatin, or blackberry fool, an English summer treat. Here you'll find cold desserts ranging from unusual fruit salads to grand soufflés, as well as hot desserts such as fritters and flambéed pineapple, with a selection of pies, tarts, and pastries to tempt even the faintest appetite.

COLD DESSERTS

Strawberry Shortcakes: Crumbly biscuits are filled with luscious strawberries and Chantilly cream, with a pool of fresh strawberry coulis all around. *Blueberry Shortcakes with Lemon Biscuits:* A hint of lemon flavors the shortcakes, which are filled with plump blueberries and cream. *Pavlova with Tropical Fruit:* Kiwi, pineapple, and mango give a tropical lilt to this giant meringue puff. *Pavlova with Mixed Berries:* This classic duo of meringue and fresh berries is named for the famed ballerina. *Summer Fruit Salad:* A decorative watermelon basket holds peaches, nectarines, cherries, melon, and assorted berries. *Exotic Fruit Salad:* Chunks of pineapple, papaya, star fruit, kiwi, mango, and lychee nuts are spiked with white wine and rum and jewelled with pomegranate seeds. *Apricot Mousse:* The delicately perfumed mousse of golden apricots is decorated with rosettes of Chantilly cream – superlative! *Strawberry Mousse with Fresh Plum Sauce:* Purple plum sauce makes a striking complement for strawberry mousse. *Cold Lemon Soufflé:* Fluffy lemon soufflé is topped with strips of candied lemon zest – a fitting end to a grand dinner. *Individual Cold Lime Soufflés:* The tang of lime lightens these chilled miniature soufflés.

Pear and Red-Currant Compote: Fresh red currants and black currant liqueur add punch to poached pears. *Nectarine Compote:* Cardamom and pistachios give poached nectarines a Middle Eastern touch. *Dried Fruit Compote:* This winter fruit dessert has orange zest and rum flavoring. *Poires Belle Hélène:* Poached pears and homemade vanilla ice cream are coated with rich chocolate sauce. *Poached Pear Fans with Chocolate Sauce:* Stylish presentation of pears in a pool of cream and chocolate sauce. *Mango Sorbet:* Refreshing ice has the rich flavor of ripe mango. *Melon Sorbet:* Aromatic cantaloupe or honeydew melon sums up the taste of summer. *Lemon Sorbet:* Served in the hollowed-out lemon shells, zesty sorbet delights children and adults alike. *Orange Caramel Creams:* Agreeably tart version of caramel custard is garnished with fresh orange. *Lime Caramel Creams:* Lime cream blends deliciously with its light caramel sauce. *Raspberry Bavarian Cake:* Rich and elegant cake has fresh raspberry Bavarian cream sandwiched between layers of sponge cake. *Orange Bavarian Cake:* Orange and Grand Marnier enliven the creamy Bavarian filling in this dessert, to be enjoyed year-round. *Blackberry Fool:* Puréed fresh blackberries, smooth pastry cream, and whipped cream make a combination to enchant us all. *Rhubarb Fool:* Refreshingly tart rhubarb with a sweet cream base has a finishing touch of candied ginger. *Red-Currant Fool:* A great way to use a tricky fruit.

HOT DESSERTS

Baked Peaches with Amaretti Cookies: A northern Italian classic fills sweet peaches with crushed almond-flavored cookies. *Baked Figs with Amaretti Cookies:* Ripe figs are stuffed to serve with orange-flavored Chantilly cream. *Raspberry Soufflé Puddings with Kirsch Custard Sauce:* An individual version of the French classic, this is made with fresh berries. *Strawberry Soufflé Pudding with Mint Custard Sauce:* Puréed strawberries are folded into meringue and baked – simple yet divine! *Fruit Fritters in Beer Batter with Fresh Orange Sauce:* Light batter coats slices of pineapple, apple, and banana. *Fruit Fritters in Champagne Batter with Raspberry Coulis:* Fritters sparkle with an effervescent Champagne batter coating. *Caribbean Flambéed Pineapple:* Tropical treat has rings of pineapple sautéed with brown sugar, pecans, and rum topped with toasted coconut. *Flambéed Bananas Foster:* This New Orleans classic combines bananas, plump raisins, cinnamon, and dark rum finished with sugar-glazed almonds. *Cherries Jubilee:* Dark sweet cherries are flambéed with kirsch and served with vanilla ice cream. *Gratin of Fresh Berries with Sabayon:* Fresh mixed berries are topped with fluffy sabayon sauce and briefly broiled. *Berries and Ice Cream with Sabayon:* The unbeatable combination of berries and ice cream heats up when topped with sabayon sauce and quickly glazed. *Gratin of Citrus Fruit and Grapes with Sabayon:* Sections of orange and grapefruit with firm grapes make a pretty winter gratin.

PIES, TARTS, AND PASTRIES

Peach Pie: Ripe peaches bake to a juicy filling, topped with a pastry lattice. *Cherry Pie:* The most famous of all American pies, made with fresh cherries, needs no introduction. *Normandy Pear Tart:* A pretty flower-shaped design of pear slices adorns this regional French tart, filled with almond cream. *Normandy Peach Tart:* Fresh peaches take the place of pears, with a jam glaze. *Phyllo Apricot Turnovers:* Triangles of phyllo enclose little bites of apricot spiced with cinnamon, nutmeg, and cloves. *Phyllo Apricot Purses:* Aromatic apricot filling is wrapped in squares of phyllo, shaped like coin purses. *Phyllo Berry Turnovers:* Lightly sweetened berries fill crisp pastry turnovers. *Caramelized Upside-Down Apple Tart:* Firm apples are cooked in caramel and served on a pastry crust, with homemade crème fraîche. *Caramelized Upside-Down Pear Tart:* Juice from pear halves combines with caramel to make a delicious topping. *Fresh Fruit Tartlets:* Colorful fresh fruit are displayed in individual pastry shells lined with pastry cream. *Fresh Fruit Tart:* A full-size tart is filled with fresh fruit, arranged in concentric circles, glistening with jam glaze. *Cherry Strudel:* Layers of flaky pastry surround fresh cherries, walnuts, brown sugar, and cinnamon in this Austrian favorite. *Dried Fruit Strudel:* Rum-soaked dried fruit and walnuts are the filling for strudel dough, served with a Chantilly cream accompaniment. *Hazelnut Torte with Strawberries:* A three-layer castle of golden-brown hazelnut pastry has strawberry and fluffy Chantilly cream filling, plus a raspberry coulis. *Almond Torte with Peaches:* Peach slices and whipped cream are layered with almond pastry – a knockout!

EQUIPMENT

Given the wide range of fruit available, and the different methods of preparing them, a variety of equipment is needed. Happily, only a few items are specialized, and in almost all cases just standard kitchen tools are required.

A chef's knife is always the best to use for slicing or cutting up fruit, particularly when it is large. Small knives come in handy for berries and small-to-medium-sized fruit. The acid in most fruit will discolor a carbon steel blade, so always use a stainless steel serrated knife or a regular blade with a high stainless content. All knives should be sharpened regularly and stored carefully to prevent dulling. The type of peeler you prefer, whether with a fixed or swivel blade, is up to you. The few special tools for cleaning and shaping fruit that you will need include a melon baller and a cherry pitter. It is also useful to have a grapefruit knife with a curved serrated blade for hollowing many small fruit.

Tart and cake pans are needed for the pies, tarts, and tortes here. It is not advisable to change the size of the pan called for in a recipe because the pastry quantity given will be wrong or the cake batter will not bake correctly. A springform pan is required for the Bavarian cake, and ramekins are needed for individual soufflés and fruit-flavored caramel creams.

Another useful piece of equipment for fruit desserts is a whisk, preferably a balloon whisk that will incorporate maximum air into whipped cream, egg whites, or sabayon sauce. For whisking egg whites, a copper bowl and balloon whisk are the classic French utensils. An electric mixer can almost always be substituted.

For piping decorations, a pastry bag with a selection of different tubes is necessary, and you will need an ice-cream maker for sorbets and any desserts with ice cream as accompaniment. At the other end of the spectrum, a deep-fat fryer is required to cook the fritters.

INGREDIENTS

Many ingredients complement fruit. A sprinkling of sugar brings out the best flavor, while a squeeze of lemon juice adds a pleasant tartness, with the added benefit of preventing fruit such as peaches and pears from discoloring. Further intensity of flavor can be added by a wide assortment of alcoholic spirits and liqueurs, such as rum, crème de cassis, and amaretto: they add that certain "something" when poaching, macerating, and flambéing.

Whipped and Chantilly cream pair happily with almost all fruit, adding richness and a contrast of color. An alternative

is pastry cream, made with milk, egg yolks, sugar, and a thickening of flour, used as a background in fruit tarts and to lighten fruit purées.

Chocolate combines luxuriously with a broad range of fruit, while gelatin is indispensable for shaping many molded desserts. As for herb sprigs and spices, they turn up in surprising places, flavoring poaching liquids and sorbets, and adding fragrance to purées. Herbs also provide a touch of fresh green decoration.

TECHNIQUES

The wide variety of fruit calls for specific techniques to deal with each one. Stone fruit is often peeled and pitted, especially in presentations calling for fruit halves and slices. The fruit is briefly scalded to loosen the skin before it is halved to remove the pit. Other fruit, such as pears and apples, need only to be peeled with a vegetable peeler before being cut into halves and/or slices.

Citrus fruit are prepared differently. The juice is often squeezed out or the fruit is peeled with a knife and then cut into sections. Zest from citrus fruit may be grated to use as a flavoring or cut into julienne and candied for decoration.

Tropical fruit, such as pineapple and mango, require individual treatment. Pineapple is peeled with a large knife to remove the skin and "eyes," while mango flesh is sliced off the pit, then scored into cubes before being cut from the skin.

Both raw and cooked fruit may be puréed to act as the foundation of a recipe or as the accompanying sauce. The techniques for cooking fruit – poaching, baking, and so on – are clearly explained here, as is the important point of judging just when fruit is done: tender but not mushy.

As with the other volumes in this series, there are many techniques for preparing other ingredients. For example, you will find how to use a vanilla bean; how to make Chantilly cream; how to make pastry leaves; how to make fruit jam glaze; how to fold mixtures together; how to stiffly whisk egg whites; how to make crème fraîche; and how to fill a pastry bag and pipe rosettes.

STRAWBERRY SHORTCAKES

 SERVES 6   WORK TIME 15-20 MINUTES   BAKING TIME 12-15 MINUTES

EQUIPMENT

metal spoons

small knife

food processor

3-inch round cookie cutter

2 round-bladed knives

large metal spoon

whisk**

strainer

metal spatula

pastry brush

bowls

wire rack

serrated knife

chopping board

baking sheet

**electric mixer can also be used

Real strawberry shortcake is made with a biscuit dough, like this rich version. A tangy strawberry coulis mingles well with the biscuits and cream.

GETTING AHEAD

Shortcake biscuits should be eaten on the day of baking and are best eaten fresh from the oven. Make the Chantilly cream not more than 2 hours ahead, and assemble the shortcakes just before serving.

SHOPPING LIST

1½ pints	strawberries
3 tbsp	granulated sugar
For the shortcake biscuits	
¼ cup	unsalted butter, more for baking sheet
2 cups	flour
1 tbsp	baking powder
½ tsp	salt
3 tbsp	granulated sugar
¾ cup	heavy cream, more if needed
For the strawberry coulis	
3 cups	strawberries
2-3 tbsp	confectioners' sugar
2 tbsp	kirsch (optional)
For the Chantilly cream	
1 cup	heavy cream
2-3 tbsp	granulated sugar
1 tsp	vanilla extract

INGREDIENTS

strawberries

heavy cream

unsalted butter

kirsch (optional)

vanilla extract

flour

baking powder

granulated sugar

confectioners' sugar

ORDER OF WORK

1 MAKE THE SHORTCAKE BISCUITS

2 PREPARE THE STRAWBERRIES AND CHANTILLY CREAM

3 ASSEMBLE THE SHORTCAKES

10

1 MAKE THE SHORTCAKE BISCUITS

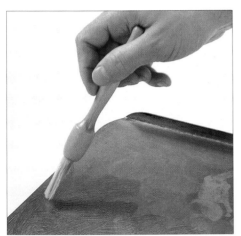

Make well in dry ingredients with your fingers

1 Heat the oven to 425° F. Butter the baking sheet.

2 Sift the flour into a large bowl with the baking powder, salt, and granulated sugar and make a well in the center.

3 Cut the butter into pieces and add to the well.

Cut with knives in scissor fashion

Cool fingers ensure dough will not be sticky

4 Cut the butter into the flour mixture using the 2 knives.

Lifting mixture while rubbing results in light pastry

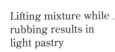

5 Rub the mixture with your fingertips, lifting and crumbling to aerate it, until it forms fine crumbs.

6 Make a well in the center, add the cream, and toss quickly with the metal spatula to form crumbs. Add a little more cream if the mixture seems dry.

! TAKE CARE !
Do not overmix or the biscuits will be heavy.

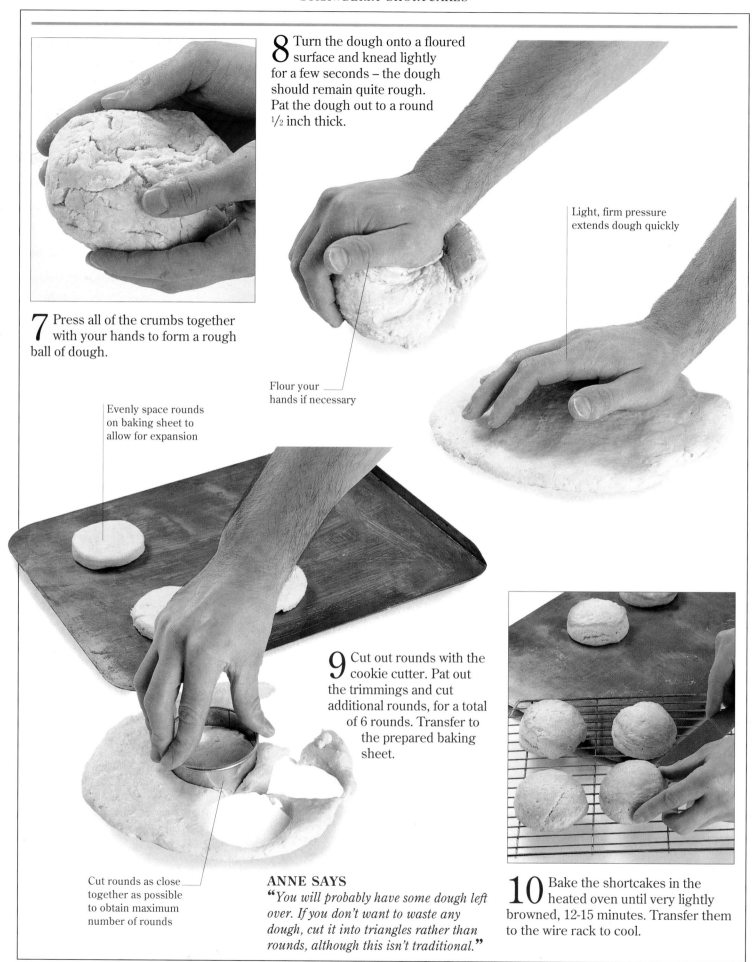

8 Turn the dough onto a floured surface and knead lightly for a few seconds – the dough should remain quite rough. Pat the dough out to a round ½ inch thick.

Light, firm pressure extends dough quickly

7 Press all of the crumbs together with your hands to form a rough ball of dough.

Flour your hands if necessary

Evenly space rounds on baking sheet to allow for expansion

9 Cut out rounds with the cookie cutter. Pat out the trimmings and cut additional rounds, for a total of 6 rounds. Transfer to the prepared baking sheet.

Cut rounds as close together as possible to obtain maximum number of rounds

ANNE SAYS
"*You will probably have some dough left over. If you don't want to waste any dough, cut it into triangles rather than rounds, although this isn't traditional.*"

10 Bake the shortcakes in the heated oven until very lightly browned, 12-15 minutes. Transfer them to the wire rack to cool.

HOW TO MAKE A BERRY COULIS

A coulis is a sauce of thickish consistency. Some of the best coulis are made with fresh berries; frozen berries can be substituted but they lack the perfume and flavor of fresh ones.

1 Hull and pick over the berries, washing them only if they are dirty. Purée the berries in a food processor or blender.

2 Transfer to a bowl. Stir in confectioners' sugar to taste and liqueur, if you like.

3 For raspberries, work the puréed fruit through a fine strainer to remove the seeds. The finished coulis should be thick enough to coat the spoon.

2 PREPARE THE STRAWBERRIES AND CHANTILLY CREAM

1 Hull the strawberries and cut into slices, reserving 6 small whole berries with hulls for garnish.

Use small knife to hull and slice strawberries

2 Sprinkle the sliced strawberries with the granulated sugar and let stand to soften, 5-10 minutes. Make a berry coulis with the strawberries, confectioners' sugar, and the kirsch, if you like (see box, left).

Make neat cuts in berry halves

3 Halve the reserved whole strawberries lengthwise, then slice just to the hull so that the halves remain intact. Press each half flat into a fan with your thumb. Make the Chantilly cream, flavoring it with the vanilla extract (see box, page 14).

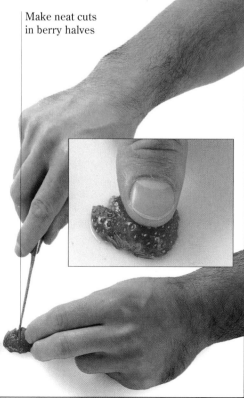

HOW TO MAKE CHANTILLY CREAM

Chantilly cream is whipped cream flavored with sugar and vanilla, brandy, rum, or a liqueur such as Grand Marnier. Only heavy cream (with minimum 36% butterfat) can be whipped, and it should be thoroughly chilled. Chantilly cream can be kept covered and refrigerated up to 2 hours. Whip the cream briefly to re-combine if it separates.

ANNE SAYS

"If the cream is to be piped, take care not to overwhip it because the cream will be worked further when it is forced through the pastry bag."

1 Pour cream into a chilled bowl. Set over ice water if kitchen is hot.

2 Whip the cream with a whisk or electric mixer until it forms soft peaks.

3 Add sugar and flavoring and whip until the cream forms soft peaks again and just holds its shape.

Whisk will leave clear marks in cream

4 Continue whipping until the cream forms stiff peaks and the whisk leaves clear marks. Do not overwhip or it will separate.

3 ASSEMBLE THE SHORTCAKES

1 Carefully cut each of the cooled biscuits in half horizontally, with the serrated knife.

! TAKE CARE !
The biscuits are quite crumbly.

2 Spoon the sliced strawberries with a little of their liquid onto the bottom halves of the shortcake biscuits. Pile the Chantilly cream on the strawberries and top each one with its lid.

3 Top each shortcake with 2 of the strawberry fans.

4 Spoon the strawberry coulis on each plate and set a shortcake in the center.

Place strawberry shortcake on coulis just before serving

Strawberry fans make pretty garnish for top of shortcake

Strawberry coulis, here flavored with kirsch, beautifully complements shortcake

V A R I A T I O N

BLUEBERRY SHORTCAKES WITH LEMON BISCUITS

This is only one of many possible variations of Strawberry Shortcakes. The lemon accents the blueberry filling. Choose blueberries that are firm and plump, discarding any that are very soft.

1 Make the shortcake biscuits as directed, adding the grated zest and juice of 1 medium lemon with the unsalted butter.
2 Make the strawberry coulis as directed.
3 Pick over 1 pint blueberries; they do not need to be sprinkled with sugar.
4 Assemble the shortcakes, piling the blueberries on top of the Chantilly cream, and decorate each with a flower or herb sprig. Serve with the coulis.

PAVLOVA WITH TROPICAL FRUIT

🍴 SERVES 6-8　　🥄 WORK TIME 25-30 MINUTES　　🍲 BAKING TIME 2-2½ HOURS

EQUIPMENT

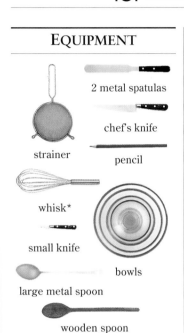

2 metal spatulas

chef's knife

strainer

pencil

whisk*

small knife

bowls

large metal spoon

wooden spoon

rubber spatula

pastry bag and
large star tube

8-inch round
cake pan

parchment paper

wire rack

chopping board

baking sheet

* electric mixer can also be used

A giant meringue puff, with a crisp outside and soft, chewy interior, filled with whipped cream and fruits. The luscious dessert is named for famous ballerina Anna Pavlova, who was a frequent visitor to Australia and New Zealand, where the dessert originated.

GETTING AHEAD

The meringue can be baked and kept up to 1 week in an airtight container. It can also be frozen. Make the Pavlova filling and Chantilly cream not more than 2 hours ahead, assembling the Pavlova just before serving.

SHOPPING LIST

5	medium kiwi fruit
1	small pineapple, weighing about 1½ lb
3	medium mangoes, total weight about 2 lb
3 tbsp	granulated sugar
2 tbsp	kirsch
	For the meringue
6	egg whites
1¾ cups	granulated sugar
1 tbsp	cornstarch
1 tsp	distilled white vinegar
	For the Chantilly cream
1½ cups	heavy cream
3-4 tbsp	granulated or confectioners' sugar
1 tsp	vanilla extract

INGREDIENTS

mangoes

pineapple

sugar

kiwi fruit

egg whites

kirsch

distilled white
vinegar

cornstarch

heavy cream

vanilla extract

ORDER OF WORK

1 MAKE THE
MERINGUE

2 PREPARE THE
PAVLOVA FILLING

3 ASSEMBLE THE
PAVLOVA

1 MAKE THE MERINGUE

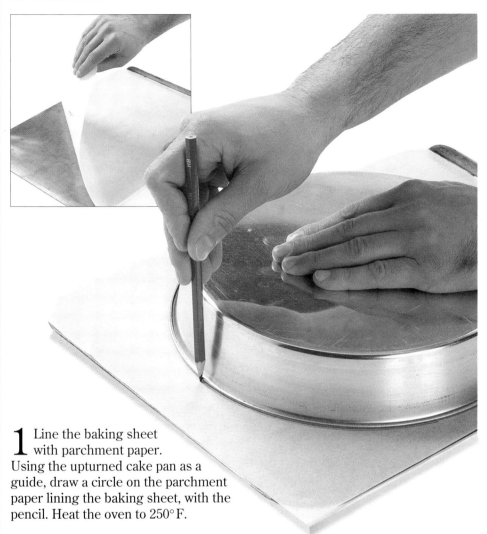

1 Line the baking sheet with parchment paper. Using the upturned cake pan as a guide, draw a circle on the parchment paper lining the baking sheet, with the pencil. Heat the oven to 250°F.

2 Whisk the egg whites until stiff (see box, right). Sprinkle in 5-6 tbsp of the sugar and continue whisking until glossy to make a light meringue, about 20 seconds. Sift the cornstarch and remaining sugar over the egg whites and add the vinegar.

3 Fold the mixture together: Cut down into the center of the bowl with the rubber spatula, scoop under the contents, and turn them over in a rolling motion. At the same time, with your other hand, turn the bowl counter-clockwise. Continue folding until thoroughly mixed.

HOW TO WHISK EGG WHITES UNTIL STIFF

Egg whites should be whisked until stiff but not dry. In order for them to whisk properly, the whites, bowl, and whisk must be completely free from any trace of water, grease, or egg yolk. A copper bowl and a large balloon whisk are the classic French utensils for whisking egg whites. A metal or glass bowl with a balloon whisk or an electric mixer can also be used.

1 Begin whisking whites slowly. When they become foamy and white, increase the whisking speed. If you like, add a small pinch of salt or cream of tartar to help achieve maximum volume.

! TAKE CARE !
Do not slow down the whisking once the whites form soft peaks or they may "turn," becoming grainy.

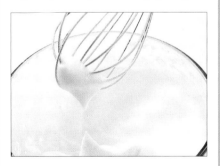

2 The whites are whisked enough if they form a stiff peak when the whisk is lifted, gathering in the whisk wires and sticking without falling. The whites should be used at once because they quickly separate on standing.

! TAKE CARE !
Do not overbeat the egg whites; the correct texture cannot be reconstituted.

6 Pile the meringue on the lined baking sheet in the center of the circle, making sure the meringue keeps within the line.

Handle carefully with metal spatulas to ensure Pavlova remains intact

7 With the back of the large metal spoon, spread out the meringue to an even round, making a deep hollow in the center. Bake the meringue in the heated oven until firm and very lightly colored, 2-2½ hours.

! TAKE CARE !
If the meringue starts to brown during cooking, lower the heat and cover it loosely with foil.

8 Let the Pavlova cool to lukewarm, then lift it off the baking sheet with 2 large metal spatulas and set it on the wire rack to cool completely. When cold, peel off the paper.

ANNE SAYS
"The exterior of the baked meringue will become crisp as it cools, while the interior stays moist and chewy."

2 PREPARE THE PAVLOVA FILLING

1 With the small knife, trim the ends of the kiwi fruit. Set the fruit upright and trim off the skin in strips, working from top to bottom.

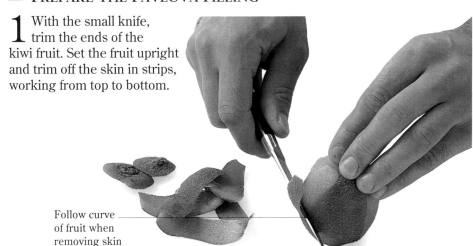

Follow curve of fruit when removing skin

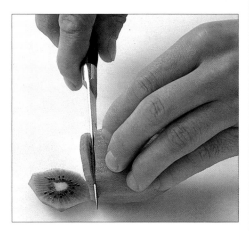

2 Cut the kiwi fruit crosswise into neat slices.

HOW TO PEEL, PIT, AND CUBE MANGO

Neatly removing the flat pit, and cubing mango, is easy if you use this method.

1 Cut each mango lengthwise into 2 pieces, slightly off-center so the knife just misses the pit. Cut the flesh away from the other side of the pit. Discard the pit.

2 Slash one piece in a lattice, cutting through the flesh but not the peel. Repeat with the other piece of the mango.

3 Holding the mango flesh upward, push the center of the peel with your thumbs to turn it inside out, opening the cuts of flesh to reveal cubes. Cut the cubes away from the skin.

Cut deep enough to remove pineapple "eyes"

3 Cut off the plume and base of the pineapple, then peel it, working from top to bottom following the curve of the fruit.

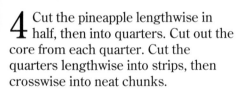

4 Cut the pineapple lengthwise in half, then into quarters. Cut out the core from each quarter. Cut the quarters lengthwise into strips, then crosswise into neat chunks.

5 Set aside a few pieces of each fruit for decoration and put the remainder in a large bowl. Sprinkle the fruit with the sugar and kirsch. Stir gently, with the wooden spoon, to distribute evenly, taking care not to break up any of the fruit pieces.

6 Make the Chantilly cream: Pour the cream into a chilled bowl and whip until soft peaks form. Add the sugar and vanilla extract and continue whipping until stiff peaks form.

Add sugar and vanilla together, once cream has formed soft peaks

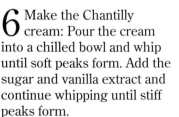

HOW TO FILL A PASTRY BAG AND PIPE ROSETTES

A star piping tube is used to pipe decorations of Chantilly cream and meringue with a professional finish.

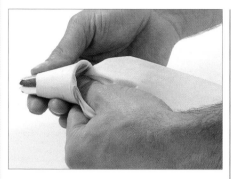

1 Drop the tube into the pastry bag and twist, tucking the bag into the tube. This will prevent any cream from leaking out at the bottom.

2 Fold the top of the bag over your hand to form a collar and add the cream or meringue, using a rubber spatula or pastry scraper and scraping it against the bag.

3 When the bag is full, twist the top until there is no air left in it. When piping, hold the twisted top of the bag between your thumb and forefinger and squeeze the bag gently to press out the cream. Do not squeeze the bag with your other hand, but simply use it to help guide the tube as you pipe.

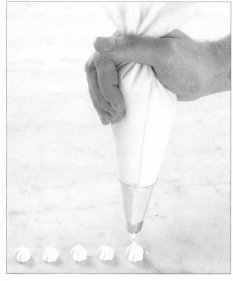

For a flower rosette: Hold the tube upright and not quite touching the surface to be decorated. Press the bag until the flower rosette is the size wanted, then stop pressing as you lift the tube upward.

For a swirled rosette: Hold the tube near the surface to be decorated. Pressing evenly, move the tube in a tight circle to form the rosette. Stop pressing before lifting the tube. For a ring of swirled rosettes or a border of rosettes: Start and stop each rosette in the same place and make them all clockwise or counterclockwise.

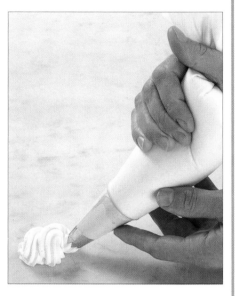

For a rope: With the tip of the tube on the surface to be decorated, pipe a swirl in a clockwise movement. Do not lift the tube, but repeat, making another swirl next to the first. Continue until the rope is completed.

For a rope of double shells: Hold the tube at a slight angle, touching the surface to be decorated. To pipe a shell, move the tube forward and then up and down, back toward you, pressing evenly. Do not lift the tube, but continue piping shells, first in one direction, then in another, until the rope is completed.

3 ASSEMBLE THE PAVLOVA

1 Put the cooled Pavlova on a serving plate and spoon in half of the Chantilly cream.

2 Arrange the mixed fruit over the Chantilly cream.

3 Put the remaining Chantilly cream into the pastry bag and pipe flower rosettes (see box, page 20) over the fruit. Arrange the reserved fruit on top and serve immediately.

Tropical fruit is framed by circle of meringue

V A R I A T I O N

PAVLOVA WITH MIXED BERRIES

Berries and meringue are a classic pair. Any variety of fresh berries can be used in place of the tropical fruit, but be sure that the berries are ripe and full of flavor.

1 Prepare the meringue as directed and put it into a large pastry bag fitted with a large star tube.
2 Starting in the center, pipe a disk of meringue inside the circle drawn on the parchment paper. Pipe a rope of double shells around the edge of the disk (see box, page 20) to form a "wall." Bake as directed.
3 Pick over 1 lb mixed berries (strawberries, raspberries, blueberries, blackberries, boysenberries), washing them only if they are dirty. Hull the strawberries. Set aside a few of each for decoration and put the rest in a large bowl. Sprinkle with 3 tbsp sugar and 2 tbsp kirsch.
4 Fill the Pavlova with the fruit and Chantilly cream as directed, piping the reserved cream on top of the fruit, in ropes radiating from the center (see box, page 20).

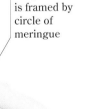

SUMMER FRUIT SALAD

🍽 SERVES 8-10 ⏱ WORK TIME 40-45 MINUTES*

EQUIPMENT

bowls

cherry pitter

small saucepan

small knife

chef's knife

metal spoon

melon baller

slotted spoon

wooden spoon

plastic wrap

chopping board

INGREDIENTS

watermelon

honeydew melon

sweet cherries

mixed berries

nectarines

Grand Marnier (optional)

freshly squeezed orange juice

peaches

sugar

When making fruit salad, the greater the variety of fruit the better, so add to the suggestions here, or substitute whatever fruit is in season. If you have any leftover fruit salad, you can serve it the next day, topped with scoops of vanilla ice cream.

GETTING AHEAD

The fruit salad can be kept in the watermelon "basket," covered, in the refrigerator 6-8 hours.

* plus 4 hours soaking time

ANNE SAYS

"*When choosing watermelon, shake to test if seeds are loose and ripe. Other types of melon should smell fragrant, and feel tender when pressed where the flower has fallen.*"

SHOPPING LIST

1	medium watermelon
6 oz	dark sweet cherries
8 oz	mixed berries, such as strawberries, raspberries, blueberries, loganberries, blackberries
1	medium honeydew, cantaloupe, or Crenshaw melon, weighing about 1¼ lb
2	large peaches
2	large nectarines
	For soaking
⅓ cup	sugar
½ cup	freshly squeezed orange juice
2-3 tbsp	Grand Marnier (optional)

ORDER OF WORK

1 **PREPARE THE WATERMELON BASKET**

2 **PREPARE THE FRUIT SALAD**

3 **SOAK AND FINISH THE FRUIT SALAD**

1 PREPARE THE WATERMELON BASKET

1 With the chef's knife, cut a thin slice from one side of the watermelon so that it sits steady on the work surface.

2 Cut vertically into the melon about 1 inch from the center of its length, cutting to the middle of the melon. Turn the melon and repeat on the other side, so that you have a 2-inch-wide band in the center.

3 From the end of the melon, cut horizontally toward the center, removing the wedge of melon. Repeat on the other side.

4 With the small knife, cut around the flesh under the "handle" in a half-moon shape and remove it.

5 Using the melon baller, cut balls from the watermelon flesh in the bottom of the basket. Remove the seeds and put the balls in a large bowl.

Shape neat balls with special cutter

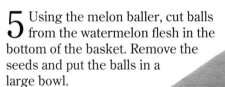

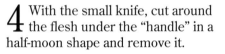

Flick out seeds with tip of small knife

6 With the metal spoon, remove the remaining bits of flesh from the melon cavity. Chill the melon basket until serving.

! TAKE CARE !
Do not pierce the bottom of the melon basket or the fruit juice will leak.

2 PREPARE THE FRUIT SALAD

1 Pit the cherries and add them to the bowl with the watermelon balls.

ANNE SAYS

"If you do not have a cherry pitter, you can scoop out the pits with the tip of a vegetable peeler."

2 Pick over the berries, washing them only if they are dirty. Hull strawberries; if they are large, halve or quarter them. Add the berries to the watermelon and cherries.

Small knife cuts hulls neatly from strawberries

3 Halve the honeydew, cantaloupe, or Crenshaw melon; scoop out and discard the seeds. With the melon baller, cut balls from the flesh, and add them to the fruit in the bowl.

Different fruit will make pretty filling

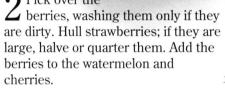

Scrape out any fibers from center of melon along with seeds

4 Immerse the peaches in boiling water in the saucepan, leave 10 seconds, then transfer with the slotted spoon to a bowl of cold water. Cut each peach in half, remove the pit, and peel off the skin. Cut each half into 6 wedges and add them to the bowl. Cut each nectarine in half, remove pit, and cut each half into 6 wedges.

3 SOAK AND FINISH THE FRUIT SALAD

1 Sprinkle the sugar over the fruit, then pour over the orange juice, and Grand Marnier, if using. Stir gently with the wooden spoon. Cover the bowl with plastic wrap and leave to soak in the refrigerator 4 hours, stirring occasionally.

! TAKE CARE !
Stir gently so you do not break up the fruit pieces.

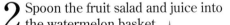

2 Spoon the fruit salad and juice into the watermelon basket. Serve chilled.

V A R I A T I O N
ALTERNATIVE MELON CONTAINERS
Any melon can be shaped as a basket or bowl for fruit salads. Here are 3 alternatives to the watermelon basket.

Melon casket with scalloped edge
1 Make a horizontal cut halfway around the top quarter of the melon. Turn uncut side toward you; cut 3 or 4 deep scallops.
2 Pull off the top of the melon; scoop out and discard the seeds and fibers.
3 Use a melon baller to scoop out balls of flesh, then scrape out the remaining flesh so that the insides of both the melon top and the base are smooth.
4 Make a cut in the flat top edge of the melon base and insert the flat edge of the melon top into the groove so that it rests over the base at an angle.
5 Mix the melon balls with other melon balls; pile them in the casket.

Melon bowl with wolves' teeth edge
1 Force the tip of a chef's knife down through the middle of the melon at a 45° angle, making a 1/2-inch slit.
2 Remove the knife and reinsert it at a 45° angle to meet the tip of the first incision. Continue in this fashion around the melon until the wolves' teeth meet at the first cut.
3 Separate the melon halves, and scoop out and discard the seeds and fibers. Fill with fruit.

Simple melon bowl
1 Choose small melons and cut each one in half. Scoop out and discard the seeds and fibers, then use a melon baller to scoop out balls of flesh.
2 With a metal spoon, scrape out the remaining flesh so that the inside of each melon half is smooth.
3 Mix the melon balls with other fruit and melon balls, and spoon into the melon bowls.

VARIATION
EXOTIC FRUIT SALAD

With modern transportation, exotic fruit are no longer restricted to their country of origin and we can enjoy different kinds of fruit from around the world all year long. They do not keep well, so buy fully ripe fruit and keep them as short a time as possible to use in this variation of Summer Fruit Salad.

1 Peel 1 small pineapple (weighing about 1½ lb), then cut it lengthwise in half and remove the core. Slice each half crosswise.

2 Cut the flesh into chunks and put them in a large bowl.

3 Cut 2 small papayas (total weight about 1 lb) lengthwise in half. Scoop out and discard the dark seeds.

4 Cut the papayas into quarters. Holding the papaya quarters with the skin side toward you, remove the skin from each quarter with a small knife.

5 With a chef's knife, cut the papaya flesh into chunks the same size as the pineapple chunks and add to the bowl.

6 Trim the ends of 3 kiwi fruit. Set the fruit upright on the work surface and trim off the skin in strips, working from top to bottom following the curve of the kiwi fruit. Cut the fruit lengthwise into quarters, then slice. Add to the bowl.

7 Cut 2 large mangoes lengthwise into 2 pieces, slightly off-center so the knife just misses the pit. Cut the flesh away from the pit. Repeat on the other side. Discard the pit. Slash the mango flesh in a lattice, not cutting through the peel, then carefully push each half inside out, opening the cuts to reveal cubes. Cut the cubes of flesh away from the skin and add them to the bowl.

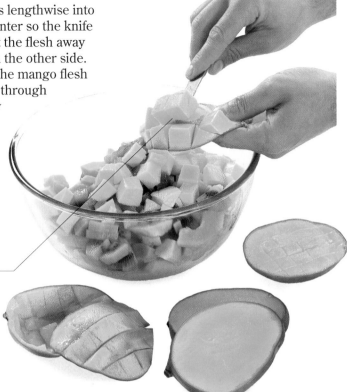

So-called "hedgehog" method of cutting away mango flesh is simple and neat

HOW TO REMOVE POMEGRANATE SEEDS

Take care when cutting into the pomegranate because if the seeds puncture the juice will leak out.

1 Using the point of a small knife, cut around the blossom end of the fruit to remove it.

2 With the tip of the knife, score the skin in quarters, taking care not to puncture any of the juicy seeds inside.

Star fruit gives decorative slices

8 Trim and discard the ends from 2 star fruit. Cut the fruit into ½-inch-thick slices and add them to the bowl. Peel 8 oz fresh lychees with your fingernail or a small knife, remove the stem end, and peel away the skin. Slit the lychee flesh on one side and remove the pit from the center. Alternatively, drain an 8-oz can of lychees. Add them to the bowl.

3 Working over a bowl, break the fruit in half using your hands, following the score lines. Break each half into quarters.

9 Remove the seeds from 1 pomegranate (see box, right) and add to the bowl. Soak the fruit salad as directed in the main recipe, replacing the orange juice with white wine and the Grand Marnier with rum.

4 Peel the hard skin back from each quarter, releasing the seeds into the bowl. Discard any pieces of membrane.

APRICOT MOUSSE

🍴 SERVES 8-10   🥣 WORK TIME 35-40 MINUTES*   ☕ POACHING TIME 10-15 MINUTES

EQUIPMENT

vegetable peeler

small knife

citrus juicer

food processor**

whisk***

strainer   wooden spoon

slotted spoon

small
heatproof
plate

parchment paper

1½-quart
ring mold

pastry bag
and small
star tube

saucepans

bowls

rubber spatula

** blender can also be used
*** electric mixer can also be used

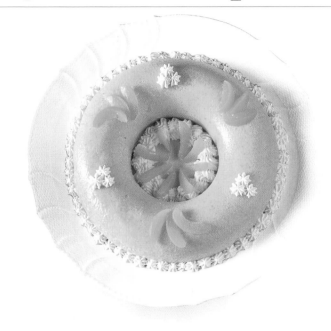

For this delicate mousse, choose fine, fresh apricots with a deep gold color, intense perfume, and soft, velvety skin.

GETTING AHEAD

The mousse can be prepared and chilled up to 24 hours ahead. Unmold and decorate not more than 1 hour before serving.

* plus at least 2 hours chilling time

INGREDIENTS

lemon

egg yolks

sugar

powdered
unflavored gelatin

apricots

kirsch

eggs

heavy cream

vanilla extract

SHOPPING LIST

For poaching the apricots	
1	lemon
1 quart	water
1 cup	sugar
For the apricot mousse	
2 lb	apricots
1 cup	heavy cream
2 tbsp	powdered unflavored gelatin
2	eggs
2	egg yolks
¾ cup	sugar
2 tbsp	kirsch
For the Chantilly cream	
½ cup	heavy cream
1-2 tbsp	sugar
½ tsp	vanilla extract

ORDER OF WORK

1 POACH THE APRICOTS

2 PREPARE THE APRICOT MOUSSE

3 UNMOLD AND DECORATE THE MOUSSE WITH CHANTILLY CREAM AND APRICOTS

1 POACH THE APRICOTS

Use indentation on apricot as guide for cutting

1 With the vegetable peeler, pare the zest from the lemon. Squeeze the juice from the lemon.

2 Halve and pit the apricots. Set aside 2 apricot halves for decoration.

3 Put the water, lemon zest, and lemon juice in a medium saucepan and add the sugar. Heat until the sugar has dissolved, then bring to a boil and cook 2 minutes.

Pour out hot mixture carefully

Hold strainer over bowl to collect poaching liquid

4 Add the apricots to the syrup. Cover them with a round of parchment paper and set the heatproof plate on top to weigh them down. Poach until very tender, 10-15 minutes.

5 Drain the apricots, reserving $1/2$ cup of the poaching liquid.

2 PREPARE THE APRICOT MOUSSE

1 Purée the apricots in the food processor; there should be about 3 cups of purée. Pour the cream into a chilled bowl and whip until it forms soft peaks, then chill it. Soften the gelatin in the reserved liquid (see box, right).

2 In the medium saucepan, whisk together the eggs, egg yolks, sugar, and apricot purée until well blended. Cook the mixture, stirring constantly, just until it boils. Pour the mixture into a large bowl and whisk thoroughly until it is light and cooled to tepid, 5-7 minutes.

3 Melt the softened gelatin (see box, right) and whisk it into the tepid apricot mixture. Continue whisking until cool.

! TAKE CARE !
The mixture must be warm when the gelatin is added or the gelatin may set instantly and form lumps.

4 Set the bowl over ice water and stir the mixture until it begins to thicken. Working quickly, fold in the whipped cream and kirsch. Cut down into the center of the bowl, scoop under the contents and turn mixture over with a rolling motion.

5 Pour the mousse into the mold. Chill until the mousse is firmly set, at least 2 hours.

ANNE SAYS
"Gelatin tends to stiffen on chilling, so let the mousse stand at room temperature about 1 hour before serving if it has been made ahead."

HOW TO SOFTEN AND MELT POWDERED GELATIN

Gelatin must be used carefully because it easily cooks into strings or forms lumps when it is added to other mixtures.

1 To soften the gelatin: Pour the water, or other liquid called for in the recipe, into a small saucepan and sprinkle the gelatin evenly on top of the liquid.

2 Let soak about 5 minutes; the gelatin will swell to a spongy consistency.

3 To melt the gelatin: Warm the saucepan over very low heat, or set it in a large bowl of hot water. Heat gently without stirring, shaking the pan occasionally. Stir the warm melted gelatin into a tepid mixture until evenly distributed.

! TAKE CARE !
Do not stir the gelatin during melting, or it may form lumps.

3 UNMOLD AND DECORATE THE MOUSSE WITH CHANTILLY CREAM AND APRICOTS

1 Run the small knife around the edge of the mold, then dip the base of the mold in a bowl of warm water for a few seconds to loosen the mousse. Dry the mold base, set a serving plate on top of the mold, and invert the mousse onto the plate.

ANNE SAYS
"If the mousse sticks, coax the sides away with your fingers."

2 To make the Chantilly cream, pour the cream into a chilled bowl and whip until soft peaks form when the whisk is lifted. Add the sugar and vanilla extract and continue whipping until stiff peaks form. Take care not to overbeat because the cream will be worked further when forced through the pastry bag. If it is too stiff, the cream will separate.

3 Fill the pastry bag with the Chantilly cream. Decorate the base and top of the mousse with small stars, and the center with a circle of continuous piping. Slice the reserved apricot halves and arrange decoratively on the mousse.

Chantilly cream is piped into stars to decorate mousse

STRAWBERRY MOUSSE WITH FRESH PLUM SAUCE

1 Substitute 2 1/2 pints strawberries for the apricots. Hull the strawberries, washing them only if they are dirty. Set aside 8 small strawberries with hulls for decoration and purée the rest in a food processor or blender.
2 Make the mousse as directed, softening the gelatin in 1/2 cup water. Fill eight 3/4-cup ramekins or molds with the mousse.
3 While the mousse is chilling, prepare a plum sauce: Halve and pit 8 oz purple plums. Poach them as for apricots. Drain the plums; reserve the poaching liquid. Purée the plums in the food processor or blender.

4 Add enough of the reserved poaching liquid to the puréed plums to make a pourable sauce.
5 Unmold each mousse onto an individual plate. Omit the Chantilly cream rosettes and top each mousse with a strawberry. Spoon some of the plum sauce around each mousse and serve the rest separately.

COLD LEMON SOUFFLE

🍴 SERVES 8   🥄 WORK TIME 35-40 MINUTES   ❄ CHILLING TIME 2-3 HOURS

EQUIPMENT

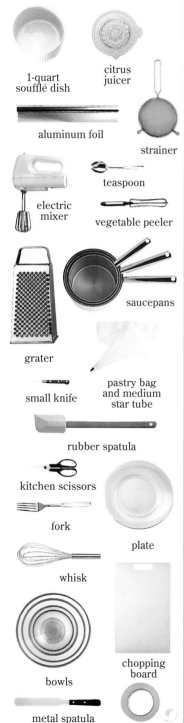

- 1-quart soufflé dish
- citrus juicer
- aluminum foil
- strainer
- electric mixer
- teaspoon
- vegetable peeler
- saucepans
- grater
- small knife
- pastry bag and medium star tube
- rubber spatula
- kitchen scissors
- fork
- plate
- whisk
- chopping board
- bowls
- metal spatula
- tape

One of the all-time best endings to a grand dinner, lemon soufflé is cool, light, and fluffy, with just the right balance of tart and sweet. Choose lemons with bright, even color and smooth rather than pitted skin.

GETTING AHEAD

The soufflé can be made, and the lemon zest candied, 1 day ahead and kept, covered, in the refrigerator. The soufflé can be decorated with Chantilly cream and candied zest, then refrigerated up to 4 hours. Remove the collar just before serving.

SHOPPING LIST

⅓ cup + ½ cup water	
1½ tbsp	powdered unflavored gelatin
4	large lemons
4	eggs
1¼ cups	sugar
1 cup	heavy cream
2	egg whites
	For the candied zest
2 tbsp	sugar
2 tbsp	water
	For the Chantilly cream
½ cup	heavy cream
1-2 tbsp	sugar
½ tsp	vanilla extract

INGREDIENTS

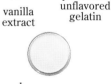

- lemons
- egg whites
- eggs
- sugar
- vanilla extract
- powdered unflavored gelatin
- heavy cream

ANNE SAYS
"Gelatin mixtures tend to stiffen on chilling, so if you prepare the soufflé ahead, let it stand at room temperature about 1 hour before serving."

ORDER OF WORK

1 PREPARE THE SOUFFLE DISH

2 MAKE THE LEMON SOUFFLE BASE

3 FINISH AND CHILL THE SOUFFLE

4 DECORATE THE SOUFFLE

1 PREPARE THE SOUFFLE DISH

1 Cut a piece of foil 2 inches longer than the circumference of the soufflé dish. Fold the foil lengthwise in half.

Fold the foil in half to increase strength

2 Wrap the foil around the dish. It should stand several inches above the rim. Secure the foil with tape.

ANNE SAYS
"So the soufflé appears to have 'risen,' the foil should reach above the rim."

2 MAKE THE LEMON SOUFFLE BASE

Sprinkle gelatin evenly over water in pan

1 Put ⅓ cup of the water in a small saucepan, sprinkle the gelatin on top, and set aside to soften until spongy, about 5 minutes.

2 Grate the zest from 3 of the lemons. Using the vegetable peeler, pare strips of zest from the remaining lemon and reserve it to candy. Squeeze the juice from all 4 lemons – there should be ⅔ cup.

3 Separate the whole eggs. In a medium saucepan, mix together the egg yolks, grated lemon zest and lemon juice, and two-thirds of the sugar until blended.

4 Cook, stirring, just until mixture boils. Pour into a large bowl and beat with the electric mixer until light and thick enough to leave a ribbon trail when the whisk is lifted, 5-7 minutes.

5 Warm the gelatin over low heat, shaking the pan, until the gelatin is melted and pourable, 1-2 minutes; do not stir. Whisk into the lemon mixture and continue whisking until cool.

3 FINISH AND CHILL THE SOUFFLE

1 Pour the cream into a chilled bowl and whip until soft peaks form; chill the cream.

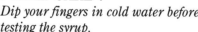

2 Heat the remaining sugar with the remaining water in a small saucepan until dissolved. Boil without stirring until the syrup reaches the hard ball stage. To test, take the pan from the heat, dip a teaspoon in the hot syrup, remove, and let cool a few seconds. Take a little syrup between your finger and thumb. It should form a firm, pliable ball.

ANNE SAYS
"If you have a candy thermometer, you can use it to test the syrup; it should register 248°F."

! TAKE CARE !
Dip your fingers in cold water before testing the syrup.

3 While the syrup is boiling, put the 6 egg whites in a bowl and whisk. Begin whisking slowly, but increase speed when they become foamy and white. Continue whisking until stiff peaks form when the whisk is lifted.

Pour syrup in thin, steady stream

4 Gradually pour the hot sugar syrup into the egg whites, whisking constantly.

Electric mixer takes over from balloon whisk

5 Continue whisking until the meringue is cool and stiff, about 5 minutes.

6 Set the bowl of lemon mixture in a larger bowl of ice water and stir the mixture gently until it starts to thicken. Remove the bowl from the ice bath.

Ice water helps mixture to thicken

Mixture will form mound when dropped from spatula

7 Fold in the whipped cream, then fold in the meringue in 2 batches (see box, right).

! TAKE CARE !
Work quickly because the mixture sets fast.

Scrape mixture from bowl with rubber spatula

Pour mixture into center of dish

8 Pour the soufflé mixture into the prepared soufflé dish – it should come at least 2 inches above the edge of the dish but below the rim of the foil collar. Chill the soufflé until firmly set, at least 2 hours.

HOW TO CUT AND FOLD MIXTURES TOGETHER

Two mixtures can be folded together most easily if their consistency is similar. If one ingredient is much lighter or more liquid than the other, such as stiffly whisked egg whites and fruit purée, first thoroughly stir a little of the lighter mixture into the heavier one to soften it.

1 Spoon one mixture over the other as directed in the recipe. With a rubber spatula, or a wooden or metal spoon, cut down into the center of the bowl.

2 Scoop under the contents, and turn them over in a rolling motion. At the same time, with your other hand, turn the bowl counter-clockwise. Continue folding gently until the mixtures are thoroughly combined.

ANNE SAYS
"This should be a synchronized movement: Cut and scoop with the spatula in one hand, turn the bowl with the other. In this way, the spatula reaches the maximum volume of mixture in one movement, so that it is folded quickly and loses a minimum of air."

HOW TO CUT AND CANDY LEMON ZEST

Candied zest adds texture and flavor to creamy desserts.

1 Cut pared zest of lemon into very fine strips.

2 Bring a small pan of water to a boil, add the zest strips, and simmer 2 minutes, then drain.

3 In the same pan, gently heat the sugar with the measured water until dissolved. Add the zest and simmer until all the water has evaporated, 8-10 minutes.

4 Remove the zest with a fork and set aside to cool.

4 DECORATE THE SOUFFLE

1 Candy the reserved lemon zest (see box, left). To make the Chantilly cream, pour the cream into a chilled bowl and whip until soft peaks form. Add the sugar and vanilla extract and continue whipping until the cream forms stiff peaks and the whisk leaves clear marks in the cream.

Kitchen scissors cut foil neatly

2 With the kitchen scissors, carefully trim the foil collar level with the top of the soufflé mixture.

Smooth cream with metal spatula

3 Spread about one-third of the Chantilly cream over the top of the soufflé.

4 With the tines of the fork, mark a lattice design in the cream.

5 Fill the pastry bag with the remaining Chantilly cream and pipe a scroll border around the edge of the soufflé.

6 Top the piped cream with the candied lemon zest.

Candied lemon zest forms a brightly colored decoration

Ease foil away gently, using small knife

¶⊙¶ TO SERVE
Carefully remove the foil collar from the soufflé. Place the soufflé dish on a serving plate.

Soufflé looks as though it has risen above the dish

INDIVIDUAL COLD LIME SOUFFLES

Lime is another favorite citrus fruit that adapts well to a cold soufflé. Look for limes that are plump, with even color and unblemished skin.

1 Instead of using a large soufflé dish, prepare eight ¹/₂-cup ramekins with foil collars, as directed.
2 Replace the lemons with 6 limes. Grate the zest from 4 of the limes and squeeze the juice from all of them.
3 Continue with the soufflé, but omit the candied zest.
4 Put 24 unsalted pistachio nuts in a bowl, cover them generously with boiling water, and let soak 5 minutes, then drain them. Rub off the skins with your fingers.
5 Decorate each soufflé with rosettes of Chantilly cream and the pistachio nuts.

PEAR AND RED-CURRANT COMPOTE

🍽 SERVES 4   🥣 WORK TIME 15-20 MINUTES*   ☕ COOKING TIME ABOUT 45 MINUTES

EQUIPMENT

whisk**

citrus juicer

fork

slotted spoon

metal spoon

small knife

vegetable peeler

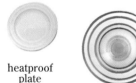
parchment paper

heatproof plate

bowls

small deep saucepan

baking sheet

**electric mixer can also be used

Here pears and red currants are flavored with vanilla and crème de cassis, topped with almonds, and served with cassis-spiked Chantilly cream. For poaching, choose fruit that is juicy and ripe, yet firm; very ripe fruit tends to break up when poached. If you cannot find crème de cassis, substitute black-currant syrup.

GETTING AHEAD

The pears and red currants can be poached up to 3 days ahead and kept, covered in their poaching liquid, in the refrigerator. Make the cassis Chantilly cream not more than 2 hours before serving.

* plus chilling time

SHOPPING LIST

4	firm pears, total weight about 1½ lb
2	lemons
1 cup	red currants
½ cup	granulated sugar
2 cups	water
2 tbsp	crème de cassis (black-currant liqueur)
1	vanilla bean or 1 tsp vanilla extract
½ cup	sliced almonds
	For the cassis Chantilly cream
1 cup	heavy cream
1-2 tbsp	confectioners' sugar
1-2 tbsp	crème de cassis (black-currant liqueur)

INGREDIENTS

pears

red currants

vanilla bean

heavy cream

crème de cassis

granulated sugar

confectioners' sugar***

sliced almonds

lemons

***granulated sugar can also be used

ORDER OF WORK

1 PREPARE THE PEARS AND RED CURRANTS

2 POACH THE PEARS AND RED CURRANTS

3 TOAST THE ALMONDS; MAKE CHANTILLY CREAM

1 PREPARE THE PEARS AND RED CURRANTS

Fork tines exert light, deft pressure

1 Peel the pears, leaving the stems intact. Cut one of the lemons in half and rub lemon juice all over the pears to prevent discoloration.

2 Working from the bottom, scoop out the seeds and core from each pear using the vegetable peeler.

! TAKE CARE !
Do not break pears open when coring.

3 Pick over the red currants and pull them from the stems with the tines of the fork.

2 POACH THE PEARS AND RED CURRANTS

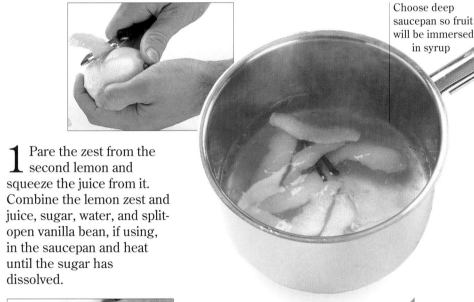

Choose deep saucepan so fruit will be immersed in syrup

1 Pare the zest from the second lemon and squeeze the juice from it. Combine the lemon zest and juice, sugar, water, and split-open vanilla bean, if using, in the saucepan and heat until the sugar has dissolved.

Test pears are tender with tip of small sharp knife

2 Bring the poaching liquid to a boil, remove the saucepan from the heat, and add the whole pears.

ANNE SAYS
"The fruit should be completely covered by syrup, so if necessary, add more water to cover."

3 Cover the fruit with a round of parchment paper and set the heatproof plate on top to weight them down. Simmer gently over low heat until the pears are almost tender, about 15-25 minutes depending on ripeness.

! TAKE CARE !
Do not let the liquid boil or the outside of the pears will disintegrate before the inside is cooked.

Be sure all stems have been removed from red currants

4 Add the red currants to the pears, return the saucepan to the heat, and continue poaching until the pears are just tender, about 10 minutes longer. Remove from the heat and test the pears are tender with the tip of the small knife.

5 Let the fruit cool in the poaching liquid, then transfer both the pears and the red currants to a glass serving bowl using the slotted spoon.

6 Boil the poaching liquid until it forms a fairly thick syrup and is reduced by about half, 5-7 minutes. Stir in the crème de cassis with the vanilla extract, if using.

7 Let the syrup cool, then strain it and pour it over the pears and red currants. Cover the compote and chill while toasting the sliced almonds and making the cassis Chantilly cream.

3 TOAST THE ALMONDS; MAKE CHANTILLY CREAM

Stir nuts occasionally so they brown evenly

! TAKE CARE !
Make sure the nuts do not burn or they will be bitter.

1 Heat the oven to 350° F. Toast the almonds in the oven, 8-10 minutes.

2 To make the Chantilly cream, pour the cream into a chilled bowl and whip until soft peaks form. Add the sugar and crème de cassis and continue whipping the cream until stiff peaks form.

🍴 TO SERVE

Sprinkle the toasted almonds over the fruit. Serve the cassis Chantilly cream in a separate bowl.

Toasted sliced almonds give crunchy texture contrast

NECTARINE COMPOTE

Nectarines marry well with cardamom, while pistachios add a pretty color contrast to this variation of pear compote.

1 Halve and pit 4 nectarines (total weight about 1½ lb); omit the pears and red currants.
2 Make the poaching syrup as directed, replacing the vanilla with 1 tsp lightly crushed cardamom pods.
3 Poach the nectarines until tender, about 5-7 minutes, then let cool in the poaching liquid before transferring to a bowl. Reduce the liquid to syrup as directed and strain.
4 To finish, omit the crème de cassis, toasted almonds, and cassis Chantilly cream. Put ¼ cup pistachio nuts in a bowl, cover generously with boiling water, and let soak 5 minutes, then drain. Rub off the skins with your fingers.
5 Sprinkle the pistachios over the nectarines and serve.

DRIED FRUIT COMPOTE

1 Pare the zest from 1 orange, then squeeze the juice from it. Bring 3 cups water to a boil with a vanilla bean, and the orange zest and juice, then add 4 oz prunes and 4 oz dried apricots. Poach the fruit 10 minutes.

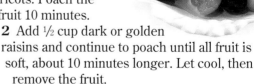

2 Add ½ cup dark or golden raisins and continue to poach until all fruit is soft, about 10 minutes longer. Let cool, then remove the fruit.
3 Add the sugar and stir until dissolved, then bring to a boil and reduce the liquid to syrup as directed. Substitute rum for the crème de cassis.
4 To finish, omit the toasted almonds and cassis Chantilly cream. If you like, pare the zest from a second orange and candy it (see box, page 36). Use the candied zest to garnish the fruit.

MANGO SORBET

 MAKES 1 QUART TO SERVE 6-8   WORK TIME 25-30 MINUTES   ❄ FREEZING TIME AT LEAST 4 HOURS

EQUIPMENT

citrus juicer

small knife

chef's knife

rubber spatula

bowls

ice-cream maker

small saucepan

ice-cream scoop

vegetable peeler

teaspoon

strainer

food processor*

chopping board

*blender can also be used

The key to good sorbet is smoothness; the ice crystals that form naturally during freezing must be forestalled. This is accomplished by stirring the mixture constantly, usually by machine. Simple and refreshing, this sorbet can be made with any number of fruit purées replacing the mango. As freezing diminishes flavor, be sure that the fruits are at their peak of ripeness. Lemon and orange juices add acid to balance sugar and heighten flavor. If you like, pour a splash of Champagne or vodka over the sorbet before serving.

GETTING AHEAD
Sorbet can be kept up to 1 week in the freezer. If frozen for more than 24 hours, let the sorbet soften in the refrigerator 30 minutes before serving.

SHOPPING LIST

½ cup	sugar, more if needed
½ cup	water
3	large, ripe mangoes, total weight 2½-3 lb
	juice of 1 lemon
	juice of 1 orange

INGREDIENTS

mangoes

orange juice

lemon juice

sugar

ANNE SAYS
"If you would like to serve sorbet ovals instead of rounds, two tablespoons can be used to shape them. Dip the spoons in cold water. Use one to scoop a generous spoonful of sorbet, scraping off the excess against the bowl. Use the second spoon to shape an oval, then let the oval fall onto a chilled plate."

ORDER OF WORK

1 MAKE THE SUGAR SYRUP

2 MAKE THE SORBET MIXTURE AND FREEZE

1 MAKE THE SUGAR SYRUP

1 Combine the sugar and water in the small saucepan.

Boil syrup until clear

2 Heat until the sugar has dissolved, then boil the syrup until it is clear, 2-3 minutes. Set aside to cool.

Let syrup cool

2 MAKE THE SORBET MIXTURE AND FREEZE

1 Peel the mangoes. Cut each mango lengthwise into 2 pieces, slightly off-center to just miss the pit. Cut the flesh away from the other side of the pit.

Work in batches so purée will be smooth

3 Purée the mango flesh in batches, in the food processor.

2 Cut the remaining thin layer of flesh from the pit. Cut all the mango flesh into cubes.

4 With all the purée in the food processor, and the blades running, pour in the cooled syrup with the lemon and orange juices. The mixture will be quite thick. Taste it, adding more sugar if it is tart.

Amount of sugar for sorbet depends on tartness of fruit

5 Pour the sorbet mixture into the ice-cream maker and freeze until firm, following the manufacturer's directions. Meanwhile, chill the bowl for the sorbet in the freezer.

ANNE SAYS
"Chilling time varies greatly with the machine you use."

Sorbet mixture should not fill container completely

Crisp cookies are perfect accompaniment

Mango sorbet is smooth and rich

6 Transfer the sorbet to the chilled bowl. Cover it and freeze at least 4 hours to allow the flavor to mellow.

🍽 **TO SERVE**
If necessary, transfer the sorbet to the refrigerator to soften slightly. Scoop the sorbet into chilled coupe glasses and serve immediately.

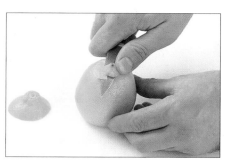

VARIATION
LEMON SORBET

*Hollowed-out lemons form
pretty individual serving dishes
for lemon sorbet.*

1 Hollow out 8 medium lemons (see box, right) to make cups. Press the lemon flesh in a strainer set over a measuring cup to extract as much juice as possible.
2 Make the sugar syrup as directed, using 2 cups water and 2 cups sugar; set aside to cool.
3 Grate the zest and squeeze the juice from 3 lemons; add to the juice in the measuring cup. If necessary, squeeze the juice from 1-2 more lemons to make 1½ cups.
4 Add the lemon juice and zest to the cooled syrup and freeze as directed. Put the lemon cups and lids on a tray and freeze them, too.

5 After the sorbet has frozen in the machine, spoon it directly into the frozen lemon cups. Mound the tops generously, add a lid, and freeze until serving.
6 Just before serving, make a small slit in each lid and insert the stem of a lemon leaf, if you have one, or a bay leaf. Put the lids on top of the sorbets.

VARIATION
MELON SORBET

*The flavor of ripe cantaloupe or honeydew melon
is heightened by the juices of lemon and lime in
this sorbet. Crisp cookies are an ideal
accompaniment.*

1 Make the sugar syrup as directed, using ¾ cup water and ¾ cup sugar; set aside to cool.
2 Halve 1 large or 2 small melons (total weight about 3 lb); scoop out and discard the seeds. Cut each half into 4 pieces and cut away the rind.
3 Purée the melon flesh in the food processor or blender and add the juice of 1 lemon and 1 lime with the sugar syrup. Freeze as directed.
4 Just before serving, scoop balls of the sorbet and pile them in chilled dessert glasses or dishes.

HOW TO MAKE LEMON OR ORANGE CUPS

*Citrus fruits are ideal for hollowing out and filling with
sorbet or fruit salad to serve in individual portions.*

1 Cut a lid from the top of each fruit, and a slice from the base so the fruit sits upright.

2 With the tip of a small knife, cut into the fruit just inside the rind to loosen the flesh.

3 Insert the knife horizontally into the bottom of the fruit, making a cut only ½ inch long. This will loosen the flesh at the bottom.

4 Scoop out the flesh into a strainer set over a measuring cup. Scrape out any remaining flesh to leave a clean hollow.

ORANGE CARAMEL CREAMS

Pudim de Laranja

¡●¡ SERVES 4   ⌣ WORK TIME 15-20 MINUTES*   ⌣ BAKING TIME 20-25 MINUTES

EQUIPMENT

small knife

chef's knife

whisk

wooden spoon

citrus juicer

plastic strainer

dish towel

small, heavy-based saucepan

4 ramekins (1 cup each)

bowls

roasting pan

chopping board

A version of caramel cream from Portugal to make your taste buds tingle, with a pretty orange color, topped with a caramel sauce. The caramel sauce should be cooked to a deep golden brown for a rich flavor, which perfectly complements the fresh tang of oranges. For maximum juiciness and sweetness, choose oranges that feel heavy in your hand and have no blemishes on the skin.

GETTING AHEAD

The orange caramel creams can be prepared, baked up to 2 days ahead, and kept in the refrigerator. Unmold them just before serving; if left to stand the caramel will discolor.

* plus 2 hours chilling time

SHOPPING LIST

	For the caramel
⅓ cup	water
½ cup	sugar
	For the orange cream
4	large oranges
5	eggs
⅓ cup	sugar
	orange slices to garnish

INGREDIENTS

oranges

eggs

sugar

ANNE SAYS
"To maintain an even heat, plain custards and creams are cooked in a water bath. They should be taken from the heat as soon as they are cooked or even a little before, because they will continue to cook in retained heat."

ORDER OF WORK

1   MAKE THE CARAMEL

2   MAKE THE ORANGE CREAM MIXTURE

3   COOK AND UNMOLD THE ORANGE CARAMEL CREAMS

1 MAKE THE CARAMEL

1 Put the water in the saucepan, add the sugar, and cook over low heat until dissolved, stirring occasionally with the wooden spoon.

2 Boil the mixture, without stirring, until it starts to turn golden.

! TAKE CARE !
Do not stir the sugar during boiling, or it may crystallize.

3 Lower the heat and continue cooking, swirling the pan once or twice so the caramel syrup colors evenly.

Caramel should be richly colored for best flavor

4 Cook until the caramel syrup is deep golden in color for best flavor. Do not overcook because caramel burns easily.

Tip and rotate ramekin to spread caramel evenly

6 Pour the caramel into the ramekins, dividing it equally among them. Working quickly, tilt each ramekin so the bottom is coated with a thin, even layer. Set the dishes aside to cool.

5 Remove the pan from the heat and immediately plunge the base of the pan into a bowl of cold water to stop the cooking.

! TAKE CARE !
The caramel is extremely hot.

2 MAKE THE ORANGE CREAM MIXTURE

1 Heat the oven to 350° F. Halve the oranges and squeeze the juice from them. There should be 2 cups of orange juice.

2 In a large bowl, whisk the eggs with the sugar until well mixed. Gently whisk in the orange juice.

3 Strain the mixture through the plastic strainer into a measuring cup so it is easy to pour.

3 COOK AND UNMOLD THE ORANGE CARAMEL CREAMS

1 Carefully pour the orange cream mixture over the caramel in the ramekins.

2 Lay the dish towel on the bottom of the roasting pan and set the ramekins on the towel.

Towel prevents water from bubbling up into creams

3 Pour hot water into the roasting pan to come more than halfway up the sides of the ramekins, to make a water bath. Bring the water to a boil on top of the stove, then transfer the pan to the heated oven.

Water bath protects delicate creams from direct heat

Small knife detaches cream from side of ramekin

4 Bake the creams until they are just set and the tip of the small knife inserted in the center comes out clean, 20-25 minutes. Take the ramekins from the hot water bath and let them cool. Chill at least 2 hours.

! TAKE CARE !
Do not overcook the creams or they will curdle.

5 Just before serving, unmold the caramel creams: Run a knife around the edge of each ramekin, then invert each cream onto a plate, allowing the sauce to pool around the cream. Serve chilled.

Caramel sauce is perfect partner for orange cream

Curled orange slice is pretty decoration

V A R I A T I O N

LIME CARAMEL CREAMS

The tangy and refreshing flavor of lime combines deliciously with a light golden caramel in this variation of Orange Caramel Creams.

1 Make the caramel as directed, cooking it to a light golden brown.
2 Make the cream mixture as directed, using the juice from 6-7 limes with 1 cup water and 1 cup sugar.
3 Decorate the unmolded caramel creams with triangular pieces of sliced lime arranged on each plate.

RASPBERRY BAVARIAN CAKE

🍽 SERVES 8   🥣 WORK TIME 55-60 MINUTES*   🍲 BAKING TIME 20-25 MINUTES

EQUIPMENT

bent metal spatula

small knife

pastry brush

food processor

electric mixer

bowls

wooden spoon

parchment paper

strainer

pastry bag and small star tube

10-inch cake pan

9-inch springform pan

wire rack

saucepans

large serrated knife

rubber spatula

metal spatula

Fresh raspberry purée flavors a Bavarian cream, sandwiched between rounds of sponge cake, and served with a kirsch-flavored custard. When raspberries are not in season you can use frozen berries, though they lack the perfume of fresh.

* plus at least 4 hours chilling time

SHOPPING LIST

For the sponge cake	
	butter, flour, and vegetable oil for pans
¼ cup	butter
1 cup	flour
	salt
4	eggs
⅔ cup	sugar
2 tbsp	kirsch
For the raspberry Bavarian cream	
1 pint	raspberries
3 tbsp	kirsch
1 cup	sugar
1 cup	heavy cream
1 quart	milk
1	vanilla bean or 2 tsp vanilla extract
10	egg yolks
3 tbsp	cornstarch
1½ tbsp	powdered unflavored gelatin
¼ cup	water
	fresh mint sprigs for decoration
For the Chantilly cream	
¾ cup	heavy cream
1-2 tbsp	sugar
1 tbsp	kirsch

INGREDIENTS

raspberries

egg yolks

sugar

unflavored gelatin

heavy cream

milk

butter

eggs

cornstarch

vanilla bean

flour

kirsch

fresh mint

ORDER OF WORK

1 MAKE THE SPONGE CAKE ROUNDS

2 MAKE THE RASPBERRY BAVARIAN CREAM

3 UNMOLD AND DECORATE THE CAKE

1 MAKE THE SPONGE CAKE ROUNDS

1 Heat the oven to 425°F. Brush the cake pan with melted butter. Line the bottom with a round of parchment paper and butter the paper. Sprinkle in 2-3 tbsp flour and turn and shake the pan to coat it evenly; tap the pan upside down to remove all excess flour.

2 Melt the butter and let it cool. Meanwhile, sift the flour and a pinch of salt into a bowl.

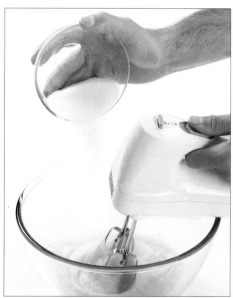

3 Put the eggs in a separate large bowl and beat a few seconds just to mix. Beat in the sugar.

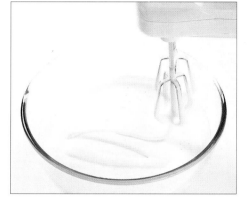

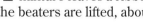

4 Beat at high speed until the mixture leaves a ribbon trail when the beaters are lifted, about 5 minutes.

ANNE SAYS
"You can use a balloon whisk instead of the electric mixer, but heat will be needed to achieve volume. Set the bowl over a pan of hot, not boiling, water, and whisk vigorously, about 10 minutes."

5 Sift about one-third of the flour mixture over the egg mixture and fold them together as lightly as possible. Add the remaining flour in the same way in 2 batches.

6 Just after folding in the flour, pour in the cooled melted butter and fold it in gently but quickly.

ANNE SAYS
"Pour melted butter in a thin, steady stream while folding it in with the rubber spatula."

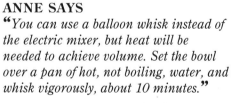

7 Pour the batter into the prepared cake pan and tap the pan on the work surface to level the batter and knock out air bubbles. Bake at once near the bottom of the heated oven, until the cake has risen and is just firm to the touch, 20-25 minutes.

Hold cake pan and wire rack together firmly

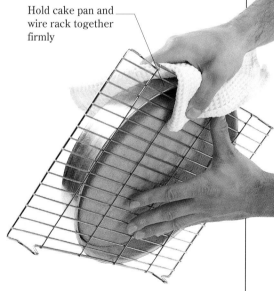

8 Turn out the cake onto the wire rack. Let cool, then carefully peel off the lining paper from the base of the cake.

9 Cut a thin slice from the top and bottom of the cake to remove the browned and marked portions; discard.

10 Cut the cake horizontally in half, using the serrated knife.

11 Trim the cake rounds to fit the springform pan, using the base of the pan as a guide.

12 Lightly oil the bottom and side of the springform pan.

ANNE SAYS

"It is best to use a good-quality stainless-steel pan for making this cake, to avoid discoloring the Bavarian-cream filling. To be extra sure, you can line the pan with plastic wrap."

13 Put one cake round in the bottom of the pan and sprinkle it with 1 tbsp of the kirsch. Set aside while making the Bavarian cream.

! TAKE CARE !

Prepare the cake and pan in advance to be ready for the Bavarian cream because it sets quickly.

Sprinkle cake evenly with kirsch

2 MAKE THE RASPBERRY BAVARIAN CREAM

Purée raspberries for Bavarian cream all at once

1 Pick over the raspberries and set aside about one-quarter. Purée the rest in the food processor or in a blender, then work the puréed fruit through the strainer to remove the seeds. There should be 1½ cups of purée. Stir in 1 tbsp of the kirsch with ½ cup sugar, or more to taste.

2 Pour the cream into a chilled bowl and whip until it forms soft peaks and just holds a shape.

3 Put the milk in a medium saucepan. Split the vanilla bean, if using, and add it to the milk. Bring just to a boil. Remove the pan from the heat, cover, and let stand in a warm place, 10-15 minutes. Remove the vanilla bean from the milk. Rinse the vanilla bean and store to use again.

4 Set aside one-quarter of the milk. Stir remaining sugar into the hot milk in the pan, until dissolved.

6 Pour the egg-yolk-and-milk mixture back into the saucepan and cook over medium heat, stirring constantly with the wooden spoon, until the custard comes just to a boil and is thick enough to coat the back of the spoon. Stir in the reserved milk and the vanilla extract, if using.

ANNE SAYS
"When the custard is thick enough, your finger will leave a clear trail across the back of the spoon."

5 Beat the egg yolks with the cornstarch in a medium bowl. Add the sweetened hot milk and whisk until the mixture is smooth.

! TAKE CARE !
Do not overwhisk or the finished custard will be frothy instead of smooth.

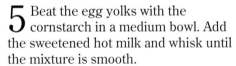

Stir melted gelatin into custard with rubber spatula

7 Strain the custard into 2 medium bowls, dividing it equally. Let cool until tepid, then stir 2 tbsp kirsch into one half. Set this kirsch custard aside to serve with the finished dessert.

8 Sprinkle the gelatin over the water in a small saucepan and let soften, about 5 minutes. Set the pan over low heat and shake it occasionally until the gelatin is melted and pourable, 1-2 minutes; do not stir. Stir into the bowl of unflavored custard.

9 Pour the raspberry purée into the unflavored custard, stirring gently until evenly mixed.

10 Set the bowl in a large bowl of ice water. Stir the mixture until it starts to thicken. Remove the bowl from the ice water immediately.

11 Fold the raspberry custard into the whipped cream.

Raspberries will sink a little into cream

12 Pour half of the Bavarian cream into the prepared pan.

13 Sprinkle the reserved whole raspberries on top, saving 8 for decoration. Pour the remaining Bavarian cream over the berries.

14 Evenly sprinkle the remaining 1 tbsp kirsch over the second cake round.

Sprinkling with kirsch ensures that cake round will be moist

15 Lightly press the cake round, sprinkled-side down, on the cream. Cover with plastic wrap and refrigerate until firm, at least 4 hours.

ANNE SAYS
"Putting the kirsch-sprinkled side of the cake on the Bavarian cream ensures the flavor is absorbed by the cream."

3 UNMOLD AND DECORATE THE CAKE

1 Take the cake from the refrigerator, uncover, and remove the side of the pan. Transfer the cake to a serving plate.

ANNE SAYS
"Use a large bent metal spatula to help move the cake off its base."

Squeeze pastry bag gently when piping

2 Make the Chantilly cream: Pour the cream into a chilled bowl and whip until soft peaks form. Add the kirsch and sugar to taste and continue whipping until the cream forms stiff peaks. Using the metal spatula, spread some of the Chantilly cream over the top of the cake.

3 Put the remaining Chantilly cream into the pastry bag and pipe it decoratively on the top of the cake.

🍽 TO SERVE
Decorate the top of the cake with the reserved raspberries and the mint and serve the kirsch custard sauce separately.

Raspberries and mint sprigs decorate Bavarian cake

—— GETTING AHEAD ——
The dessert can be made up to 48 hours ahead and kept in the refrigerator; remove 1 hour before serving. Make the Chantilly cream not more than 2 hours before serving.

V A R I A T I O N

ORANGE BAVARIAN CAKE

In this year-round variation of Raspberry Bavarian Cake, the Bavarian cream is flavored with orange zest and juice, with a piquant hint of Grand Marnier.

1 Make the sponge cake rounds and prepare the springform pan as directed, sprinkling the first cake round with 1 tbsp Grand Marnier.
2 Grate the zest from 1 orange and squeeze the juice from 3 oranges (there should be 1 cup juice). Whip the cream, and soften 2 tbsp powdered unflavored gelatin in ¼ cup of the orange juice.
3 Make the custard sauce and divide it between 2 bowls. Stir 1 tbsp Grand Marnier into one half of the custard and set it aside for serving. Melt the gelatin and stir it into the unflavored custard sauce with the remaining orange juice, the zest, and 1 tbsp Grand Marnier. Continue with the Bavarian cream as directed.
4 Finish the cake as directed, sprinkling the remaining cake round with 1 tbsp Grand Marnier.
5 Peel and section 2 oranges, cutting down between the membranes. Unmold the cake and spread with all of the Chantilly cream. Decorate with the orange sections and serve the Grand Marnier custard sauce separately.

BLACKBERRY FOOL

🍽 SERVES 8   🥣 WORK TIME 20-25 MINUTES   ❄ CHILLING TIME 2 HOURS

EQUIPMENT

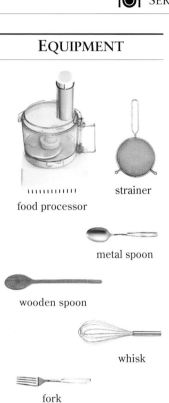

food processor

strainer

metal spoon

wooden spoon

whisk

fork

saucepans

bowls

rubber spatula

The name "fool" for this English dessert dates back at least to the sixteenth century and probably comes from the French "fouler," meaning to purée a mixture. Fools are traditionally made with a tart fruit.

— GETTING AHEAD —

The fool can be made 2 days in advance and the flavor will mellow. Keep it, covered, in the refrigerator.

SHOPPING LIST

1 lb	blackberries
1/4 cup	water
4-5 tbsp	sugar, more if needed
1 cup	heavy cream
	fresh mint sprigs for decoration
	For the pastry cream
1 1/2 cups	milk
1	vanilla bean or 2 tsp vanilla extract
5	egg yolks
1/3 cup	sugar
1/4 cup	flour
1/2 tbsp	unsalted butter

INGREDIENTS

blackberries

sugar

heavy cream

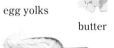

milk

vanilla bean

egg yolks

butter

flour

fresh mint

ORDER OF WORK

1 **PREPARE THE BLACKBERRY PURÉE**

2 **MAKE THE PASTRY CREAM**

3 **FINISH THE FOOL**

1 PREPARE THE BLACKBERRY PURÉE

1 Pick over the blackberries and set aside 8 for decoration. Put the berries in a saucepan with the water.

2 Simmer over medium heat, stirring, until soft, but of a thick consistency, 8-10 minutes.

3 Transfer the berries and liquid to the food processor and purée to a fairly coarse texture.

Use wooden spoon to press purée through strainer

4 Press the purée through the strainer to remove the seeds. There should be 1½ cups of purée.

5 Stir in sugar to taste and set the purée aside to cool.

ANNE SAYS
"Flavors will blend and develop as the purée cools."

2 MAKE THE PASTRY CREAM

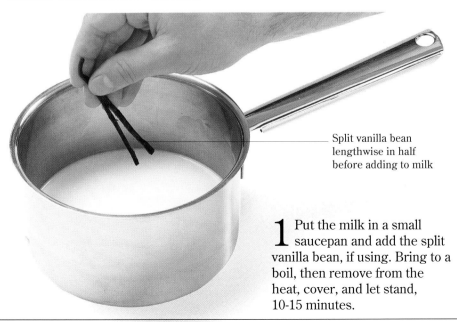

Split vanilla bean lengthwise in half before adding to milk

1 Put the milk in a small saucepan and add the split vanilla bean, if using. Bring to a boil, then remove from the heat, cover, and let stand, 10-15 minutes.

2 In a large bowl, whisk the egg yolks, sugar, and flour just to mix.

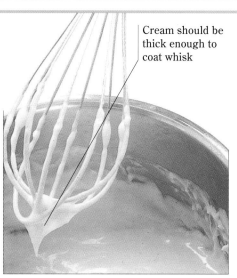
Cream should be thick enough to coat whisk

3 Whisk the hot milk into the egg-yolk mixture until all the ingredients are thoroughly combined.

4 Return the mixture to the pan and cook over low heat, whisking constantly, until the flour has cooked and the pastry cream has thickened, 2-3 minutes. Simmer the cream over low heat 2 minutes longer.

5 Transfer the pastry cream to a bowl and remove the vanilla bean, if using, or stir in the vanilla extract. Using the fork, rub the butter over the surface of the cream to prevent a skin from forming. Set aside to cool.

3 FINISH THE FOOL

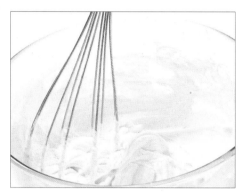

Rubber spatula is excellent for folding mixtures together

1 Pour the cream into a chilled bowl and whip until stiff peaks form and the whisk leaves clear marks in the cream. Set aside.

ANNE SAYS
"If the kitchen is hot, set the bowl over ice water."

2 Add the blackberry purée to the cooled pastry cream and stir in with the rubber spatula to mix thoroughly.

3 Fold in the whipped cream. Cut down into the center with the spatula, scoop under contents and turn over in a rolling motion. Taste; add more sugar if necessary.

4 Spoon the fool into stemmed glasses. If you like, mark a pattern on the surface of each fool. Cover and chill at least 2 hours.

Spoon fool into center of glass to keep rim clean

¡●¡ TO SERVE

Decorate each fool with a blackberry and a mint sprig and serve chilled.

Fresh mint leaves give additional piquancy

Pretty color of fool is shown off in elegant stemmed glass

RED-CURRANT FOOL

Red currants are a natural for a fool, with cranberries an alternative autumn possibility. Both need more sugar than blackberries, so be sure to taste the fruit purée after adding the pastry cream.

1 Pick over 1 lb red currants or cranberries. If using red currants, set aside 8 small bunches for garnish and pull the stems from the remaining currants with the tines of a fork.
2 Simmer the fruit with the water as directed until soft, 6-8 minutes. Continue as directed, adding more sugar to taste.
3 Spoon the fool into stemmed glasses and chill.
4 Top with the reserved currants and tiny mint sprigs, or sprinkle cranberry fool with ground cinnamon to serve.

RHUBARB FOOL

The tartness of rhubarb is ideal for fools. Strips of candied ginger make an attractive decoration, with crisp brandy snap cookies on the side.

1 Trim 12 oz rhubarb stalks and wash them thoroughly.
2 Cut the stalks into 1-inch pieces. Simmer with the water as directed until tender, 10-12 minutes. The coarse texture of the fruit is important in this dessert: Do not purée the rhubarb. Stir in ½ cup sugar; add more if needed, to taste.
3 With a fork, crush the rhubarb against the side of the pan. Transfer the rhubarb to a bowl. Continue as directed.
4 Decorate the fools with candied ginger, if you like. Serve chilled in stemmed glasses.

POIRES BELLE HELENE

EQUIPMENT

slotted spoon

ice-cream maker

vegetable peeler

heavy-based saucepans, 1 with lid

small ladle

large shallow pan

kitchen scissors

ice-cream scoop

wooden spoon

whisk

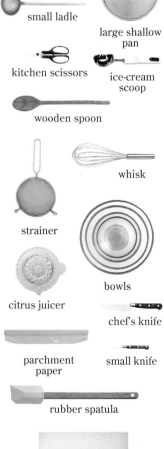

strainer

citrus juicer

bowls

chef's knife

parchment paper

small knife

rubber spatula

chopping board

This dessert of poached pears, vanilla ice cream, and hot chocolate sauce dates from the nineteenth century, when it was created for the star of Offenbach's opera, "La Belle Hélène."

GETTING AHEAD

A good dessert to prepare ahead: The ice cream can be made and frozen up to 2 weeks in advance. The chocolate sauce can be refrigerated, and the pears kept, covered in their poaching liquid, in the refrigerator, up to 3 days.

plus 4 hours freezing time

SHOPPING LIST

2	lemons
6	firm pears, total weight about 1½ lb
3 cups	water
1	vanilla bean
¾ cup	sugar
	fresh mint sprigs for decoration
	For the vanilla ice cream
2½ cups	milk
1	vanilla bean
½ cup + 2 tbsp	sugar
8	egg yolks
2 tbsp	cornstarch
1 cup	heavy cream
	For the chocolate sauce
8 oz	semisweet chocolate
½ cup	water
1 tbsp	brandy

INGREDIENTS

pears

fresh mint sprigs

semisweet chocolate

sugar

vanilla beans

brandy

milk

egg yolks

heavy cream

lemons

cornstarch

ORDER OF WORK

1 MAKE THE ICE CREAM

2 POACH THE PEARS

3 MAKE THE CHOCOLATE SAUCE AND FINISH THE DISH

1 MAKE THE ICE CREAM

1 Put the milk in a medium saucepan. Split the vanilla bean (see box, page 63) and add it to the milk. Bring the milk just to a boil. Remove from the heat, cover, and let stand in a warm place, 10-15 minutes. Remove the vanilla bean.

2 Set aside one-quarter of the flavored milk. Add the sugar to the remaining flavored warm milk and stir, with the wooden spoon, until all the sugar has dissolved.

3 Put the egg yolks with the cornstarch into a medium bowl. Whisk them together until the mixture is smooth.

Pour in flavored milk while whisking

Dish towel keeps bowl steady while whisking

4 Pour the sweetened flavored milk into the egg-yolk mixture, whisking until just smooth.

! TAKE CARE !
Do not overwhisk or the finished custard will be frothy instead of smooth.

5 Cook the custard over medium heat, stirring constantly with the wooden spoon, until it comes just to a boil and thickens enough to coat the back of the spoon. Your finger will leave a clear trail across the spoon.

! TAKE CARE !
Do not continue to boil the custard or it may curdle.

Straining ensures custard is smooth

6 Add the reserved flavored milk to the custard and stir continuously with the wooden spoon to combine, until it comes back to a boil.

7 Strain the custard into a cold bowl and leave it to cool completely. If it forms a skin, whisk to dissolve it.

8 Pour the vanilla custard into the ice-cream maker and freeze until slushy, following the manufacturer's directions. Meanwhile, chill a large bowl in the freezer.

9 Pour the cream into another chilled bowl and whip until soft peaks form.

Rubber spatula is efficient tool for transferring cream

10 Add the whipped cream to the half-set vanilla custard and continue freezing until firm.

Ice-cream maker will mix cream into custard

11 Transfer the ice cream to the chilled bowl, cover it, and freeze at least 4 hours. If you make the ice cream well ahead of time, put it in the refrigerator to let it soften, about 30 minutes before scooping.

2 POACH THE PEARS

1 Cut one of the lemons in half. Peel a pear, leaving the stem intact.

2 Rub the cut surface of the lemon all over the peeled pear to prevent discoloration.

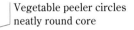

Vegetable peeler circles neatly round core

3 Working from the bottom, scoop out the seeds and membrane from the pear using the vegetable peeler, without breaking open the fruit. Repeat with the remaining pears.

Intact stem preserves character of pear

HOW TO SPLIT AND USE A VANILLA BEAN

Vanilla beans are used to flavor hot liquids such as milk and sugar syrup. They should be split open before use, so the vanilla seeds are exposed.

Thinly pared zest leaves pith behind

4 Pare the zest from the second lemon with the vegetable peeler. Squeeze the juice from the lemon.

With a small sharp knife, cut the vanilla bean lengthwise in half to expose the flavorful seeds. Add the bean to the liquid and bring it just to a boil. Remove from heat, cover and let stand 10-15 minutes. To give a stronger vanilla flavor, remove the bean from the liquid, scrape out the seeds onto a board, and then return the seeds to the liquid and let stand 10 minutes more. Rinse the vanilla bean, dry, and store to use again.

5 Make the poaching syrup: Combine the water, vanilla bean, if using, lemon zest and juice, and sugar in the shallow pan.

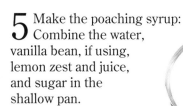

Add sugar all at once

Use pan that will hold all pears in single layer

6 Heat the mixture until the sugar has dissolved, then bring to a boil.

7 Remove the pan from the heat. Add the whole pears to the poaching syrup.

ANNE SAYS
"The pears should be completely covered by syrup, so if necessary add more water to cover them."

Discard parchment paper once pears are cooked

8 Cut a disk of parchment paper the same diameter as the pan. Dampen it, then place it on top of the pears to keep them submerged in the syrup.

Do not cut into pears too deeply when testing if tender

9 Simmer the pears gently over low heat until tender when pierced with a small knife, 25-35 minutes, depending on ripeness. Let the pears cool in the liquid.

! TAKE CARE !
Do not let the liquid boil or the outside of the pears will disintegrate before the inside is cooked.

3 MAKE THE CHOCOLATE SAUCE AND FINISH THE DISH

1 Cut the chocolate into large chunks. Chop them with the chef's knife or in a food processor, using the pulse button. Combine the water and chocolate in a small saucepan. Stir over gentle heat until the chocolate is melted and smooth.

2 Simmer until slightly thickened and the consistency of heavy cream, 2-3 minutes. Remove from the heat, stir in the brandy, and keep the sauce warm.

3 Drain the pears well. Set a pear in the center of each of 6 chilled serving plates. Arrange 5 scoops of vanilla ice cream around each pear. Ladle some warm chocolate sauce over the pears, decorate with mint, and serve at once. Pass the remaining sauce separately.

Warm chocolate sauce runs smoothly onto pear

Poached pear looks attractive with chocolate sauce poured sparingly on top

Mint leaves introduce green accent

VARIATION

POACHED PEAR FANS WITH CHOCOLATE SAUCE

Pear "fans" make a pretty presentation on a pool of cream, with chocolate sauce as a finishing touch.

1 Poach the pears and make the chocolate sauce as directed; omit the vanilla ice cream.
2 Cut each pear lengthwise in half, then cut each half lengthwise into slices, keeping the slices attached to the stem. Press down gently with your fingertips on each pear half to separate the slices slightly.
3 Spoon 2-3 tbsp heavy cream onto 6 dessert plates and tilt them to spread out the cream into a pool. Arrange 2 pear halves on each plate, fanning out the slices.
4 Drizzle sauce in a wavy line onto each plate. To feather, draw the tip of a small knife across at intervals.

5 Spoon some chocolate sauce onto each pear half, near the stem.

BAKED PEACHES WITH AMARETTI COOKIES

 SERVES 6   WORK TIME 15-20 MINUTES   BAKING TIME 1-1¼ HOURS

EQUIPMENT

slotted spoon

small knife

food processor   metal spoon

whisk*

bowls   medium saucepan

baking dish

chopping board

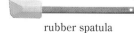

rubber spatula

A classic dessert from northern Italy, as delicious as it is easy to prepare, this can be served hot or cold. Amaretti cookies, with their hint of bitter almonds, pick up the sweetness of the peaches, but macaroons can be substituted. The peaches should be ripe and full of juice, with no green tinge, or bruised or wrinkled skin.

GETTING AHEAD

The peaches can be baked ahead and kept up to 1 day in the refrigerator. Serve them cold, or cover and reheat them in a 350° F oven about 15 minutes.

SHOPPING LIST

7	large, ripe yellow peaches, total weight about 2lb
8-10	Amaretti cookies
⅓ cup	sugar
1	egg yolk
	unsalted butter for baking dish
	fresh mint sprigs for decoration
	For the Chantilly cream
½ cup	heavy cream
1-2 tbsp	sugar
1-2 tbsp	Amaretto liqueur

INGREDIENTS

peaches

Amaretti cookies   unsalted butter

sugar

egg yolk

heavy cream   Amaretto liqueur*

fresh mint sprigs

* kirsch can also be used

ORDER OF WORK

1 PREPARE THE FILLING

2 PREPARE, FILL, AND BAKE THE PEACHES

* electric mixer can also be used

1 PREPARE THE FILLING

Use metal blade in food processor

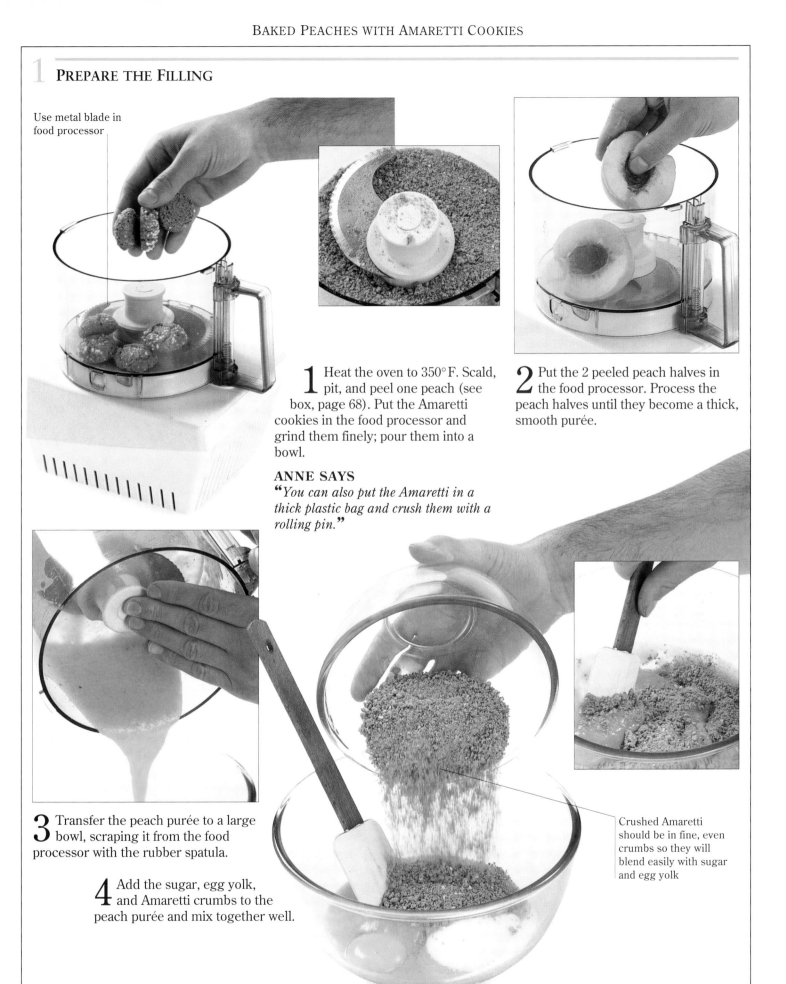

1 Heat the oven to 350° F. Scald, pit, and peel one peach (see box, page 68). Put the Amaretti cookies in the food processor and grind them finely; pour them into a bowl.

ANNE SAYS
"You can also put the Amaretti in a thick plastic bag and crush them with a rolling pin."

2 Put the 2 peeled peach halves in the food processor. Process the peach halves until they become a thick, smooth purée.

3 Transfer the peach purée to a large bowl, scraping it from the food processor with the rubber spatula.

4 Add the sugar, egg yolk, and Amaretti crumbs to the peach purée and mix together well.

Crushed Amaretti should be in fine, even crumbs so they will blend easily with sugar and egg yolk

HOW TO SCALD, PIT, AND PEEL A PEACH

1 Bring a small saucepan of water to a boil. Using a slotted spoon, immerse the peach in the boiling water, about 10 seconds.

2 With a slotted spoon, transfer the peach to a bowl of cold water.

ANNE SAYS
"This loosens the skin. If peaches are less ripe, leave in the boiling water longer."

3 With a small knife, cut the peach in half, using the indentation on one side of the peach as a guide.

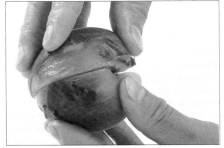

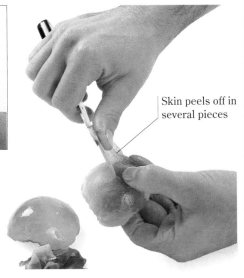

Skin peels off in several pieces

4 Using both hands, give a quick, sharp twist to each half to loosen it from the pit.

ANNE SAYS
"If the peach clings, loosen the flesh from the pit with a knife."

5 Lift or scoop out the pit with a small knife and discard it.

6 Peel off the skin from the peach halves.

2 PREPARE, FILL, AND BAKE THE PEACHES

1 Butter the baking dish. Halve and remove the pit from the remaining peaches without peeling them. If necessary, with a spoon, scoop out a little of the peach flesh from the center of each half so the cavity is large enough to hold the filling.

Use sharp-edged spoon to hollow out peach halves ready for filling

2 Set the peach halves, cut-side up, in the baking dish. Spoon some of the filling into each peach.

ANNE SAYS
"The peaches should fit tightly in the buttered baking dish."

HOW TO MAKE CHANTILLY CREAM

Chantilly cream is whipped heavy cream, lightly sweetened with sugar and flavored with vanilla, brandy, kirsch, or other liqueurs and flavorings.

Pour the cream into a chilled bowl and whip until soft peaks form. Add the sugar and flavoring, and continue whipping until the cream forms stiff peaks.

🍽 TO SERVE

Transfer the hot peaches to individual serving plates, spoon any juices over the peaches, and decorate with mint sprigs. Serve the Chantilly cream in a separate bowl.

3 Bake the peaches in the heated oven until the peaches are tender, 1-1¼ hours. Meanwhile, make the Chantilly cream (see box, left).

Test peaches for tenderness by piercing flesh with tip of small knife

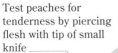

Amaretto and peach filling is bittersweet

V A R I A T I O N

BAKED FIGS WITH AMARETTI COOKIES

Look for ripe figs with a sweet smell and no blemishes, for this variation.

1 With a small knife, trim the stem ends off 14 ripe but firm, purple figs (total weight about 2 lb).

2 Peel the skin from 2 of the figs using a small knife and purée the figs. Make the filling as directed, using the puréed figs and 6-8 Amaretti cookies.

3 Cut a deep cross in the tops of the remaining figs, and open them by pushing the sides slightly.
4 Fill the figs and bake as directed, allowing 40-45 minutes.
5 Flavor the Chantilly cream with about 3 tbsp orange juice and 1-2 tbsp Grand Marnier or other orange liqueur.
6 Allowing 2 per person, serve the figs hot, with the orange Chantilly cream.

RASPBERRY SOUFFLE PUDDINGS WITH KIRSCH CUSTARD SAUCE

  SERVES 6   WORK TIME 20-25 MINUTES BAKING TIME 10-12 MINUTES

EQUIPMENT

6 medium ramekins
(1 cup capacity)

bowl strainers   conical strainer

pastry brush

whisk

wooden spoon

small ladle

heavy-based
saucepan

food processor*

bowls

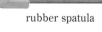
rubber spatula

baking sheet

* blender can also be used

A hot, baked soufflé, and particularly this pudding version, need not be intimidating. What could be simpler than puréed fruit folded into meringue and baked? Here the puddings are served with a chilled custard sauce flavored with kirsch. Given the few ingredients of this recipe, it is important that the raspberries be as sweet, juicy, and highly flavored as possible.

GETTING AHEAD
The raspberry purée and kirsch custard sauce can both be prepared up to 1 day in advance and kept, covered, in the refrigerator. The egg whites must be whisked and the puddings baked just before serving.

SHOPPING LIST

	unsalted butter and granulated sugar for ramekins
1 pint	raspberries
½ cup	granulated sugar, more if needed
5	egg whites
2-3 tbsp	confectioners' sugar for sprinkling
	For the kirsch custard sauce
1½ cups	milk
¼ cup	granulated sugar
5	egg yolks
1 tbsp	cornstarch
2-3 tbsp	kirsch

INGREDIENTS

raspberries

cornstarch   kirsch

milk

egg yolks   egg whites

confectioners'
sugar

butter

granulated
sugar

ORDER OF WORK

1 MAKE THE KIRSCH CUSTARD SAUCE

2 PREPARE AND BAKE THE PUDDINGS

1 MAKE THE KIRSCH CUSTARD SAUCE

1 Pour the milk into the heavy-based saucepan and bring just to a boil over medium heat.

2 Set aside one-quarter of the milk to add later. Add the sugar to the remaining hot milk and stir until dissolved.

3 Put the egg yolks with the cornstarch, into a medium bowl. Whisk them together lightly, until the mixture is smooth.

4 Add the sweetened milk to the egg yolks, whisking until just smooth.

ANNE SAYS
"Do not overwhisk or the custard will be frothy instead of smooth."

Straining ensures custard is smooth

5 Cook the custard over medium heat, stirring constantly, until it comes just to a boil and thickens enough to coat the back of the spoon. Remove from heat. Your finger will leave a clear trail across the spoon.

! TAKE CARE !
Do not continue to boil the custard or it may curdle.

6 Stir the reserved milk into the custard, then strain it into a cold bowl and let it cool. If it forms a skin, whisk to dissolve it. Stir in the kirsch. Cover the custard tightly and refrigerate it while preparing and baking the soufflé puddings, about 25 minutes.

2 PREPARE AND BAKE THE PUDDINGS

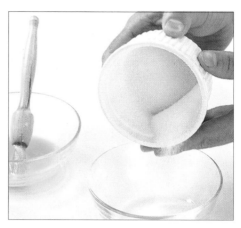

1 Brush the ramekins with melted butter. Sprinkle each dish with granulated sugar, tilting to coat the bottoms and sides evenly, and tip out excess sugar. Heat the oven to 375°F.

2 Pick over the raspberries, then purée them with half of the granulated sugar in the food processor. Taste and add more sugar if the purée is tart.

3 Using the small ladle, work the purée through the conical strainer into a large bowl to remove the seeds.

4 Whisk the egg whites until stiff. Sprinkle in the remaining granulated sugar and continue whisking until glossy to form a light meringue, about 20 seconds.

Raspberry-meringue mixture should have same texture as remaining meringue to make folding easy

5 Add about one-quarter of the meringue to the raspberry purée and stir the two together lightly, with the rubber spatula, to combine.

6 Add this mixture to the remaining meringue and fold together; cut down into the center of the bowl with the rubber spatula, scoop under the contents and turn them over in a rolling motion.

7 Continue folding until the meringue is thoroughly incorporated into the raspberry purée and the mixture is an even color.

Divide mixture evenly among ramekin dishes

8 Spoon the pudding mixture into the prepared ramekins. Set them on a baking sheet for easy handling. Bake in the oven until they are puffed and lightly browned on top, 10-12 minutes. Sprinkle the soufflé puddings with the confectioners' sugar, using the strainer, and serve immediately, accompanied by the kirsch custard sauce.

Kirsch-flavored custard sauce makes a delicate accompaniment

Confectioners' sugar lightly dusted on top is finishing touch

V A R I A T I O N

STRAWBERRY SOUFFLE PUDDING WITH MINT CUSTARD SAUCE

Another red berry takes the stage here. If desired, make a diamond template to pattern the pudding with sugar.

1 Lightly crush a small bunch of fresh mint to develop the flavor.
2 Make the custard sauce, adding the mint to the hot milk, covering, and letting stand in a warm place, 10-15 minutes. Omit the kirsch.
3 Hull 1 pint strawberries, washing them only if they are dirty, and purée them with sugar as directed. There is no need to strain the purée.
4 Prepare the pudding mixture as directed, using the strawberry in place of the raspberry purée, and bake in a prepared 1½-quart soufflé dish, allowing 15-20 minutes.
5 Serve immediately, with the mint custard sauce alongside.

FRUIT FRITTERS IN BEER BATTER WITH FRESH ORANGE SAUCE

🍴 SERVES 6-8   🥣 WORK TIME 20-30 MINUTES   ☕ FRYING TIME 30-35 MINUTES

EQUIPMENT

whisk*

2-pronged fork

vegetable peeler   apple corer

deep-fat
thermometer
if needed

small round
cookie
cutter

slotted spoon

chef's knife

paper towels

small saucepan

large metal spoon

strainer   bowls

deep-fat fryer**   chopping board

baking sheet

*electric mixer can also be used
**large pot can also be used

A light coating of batter allows fruit to be deep-fried while retaining its flavor and juice. The beer in the batter gives an especially crisp coating.

GETTING AHEAD

The fruit, batter, and sauce can be prepared and kept, covered, in the refrigerator up to 6 hours. Add the whisked egg whites to the batter and fry just before serving.

SHOPPING LIST

1	pineapple, weighing about 2 lb
4	tart apples, total weight about 1½ lb
2	ripe bananas
	oil for deep-frying
3-4 tbsp	confectioners' sugar for serving
	For the batter
1 cup	flour
	salt
1	egg
½ cup	beer, more if needed
2	egg whites
2 tbsp	granulated sugar
1 tbsp	vegetable oil
	For the fresh orange sauce
3	oranges
¼ cup	orange marmalade
1 tbsp	granulated sugar (optional)

INGREDIENTS

oranges   bananas

beer

apples

pineapple   egg

flour

granulated sugar

confectioners'
sugar

orange marmalade

vegetable
oil   egg whites   oil for
deep-frying

ORDER OF WORK

1 MAKE THE BATTER

2 MAKE THE FRESH
ORANGE SAUCE

3 PREPARE THE FRUIT

4 DEEP-FRY THE
FRITTERS

1 MAKE THE BATTER

1 Sift the flour into a large bowl using the strainer or a flour sifter. Add the salt and make a well in the center.

2 Add the whole egg and half of the beer to the well in the flour.

ANNE SAYS
"If too much liquid is added at this point, the batter will form lumps."

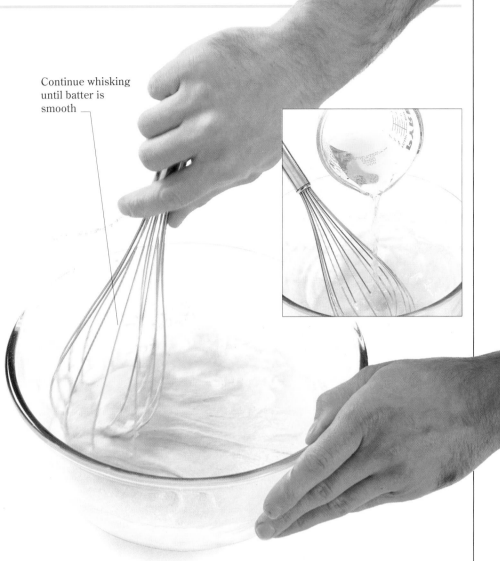

Continue whisking until batter is smooth

3 Mix with the whisk to make a smooth paste. Mix in the remaining beer. Cover and let stand at least 30 minutes.

ANNE SAYS
"The batter will thicken on standing."

2 MAKE THE FRESH ORANGE SAUCE

1 With the vegetable peeler, pare the zest from one of the oranges. Cut the zest into thin strips.

Use chef's knife to thinly cut strips

2 Put the zest in the small pan and add water to cover it generously. Bring to a boil and simmer 2 minutes. Drain, rinse under cold water, and drain again. Transfer to a bowl.

HOW TO PEEL AND SECTION CITRUS FRUIT

Seedless citrus fruit, such as navel oranges, are best for cutting into sections.

1 With a chef's knife, cut away both ends of the fruit just to the flesh. Set the fruit upright on a chopping board. Working from top to bottom using the same knife, cut away the zest, pith, and skin following the curve of the fruit.

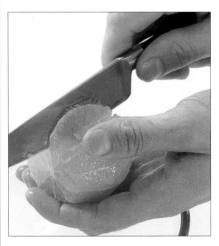

2 Holding the fruit in your hand, slide the knife down one side of a section, cutting the section from the membrane. Cut down the other side and pull out the section. Repeat with remaining sections, turning back flaps of membrane like the pages of a book.

ANNE SAYS

"Section the fruit over a bowl to catch the juice."

Tip orange sections and juice into bowl of orange zest

Orange sections should be free of all pith

3 Peel all 3 oranges with the chef's knife; working over a bowl, section the oranges (see box, left), reserving the juice. Add the sections to the strips of orange zest.

4 Put the marmalade and orange juice in the small saucepan.

5 Heat gently until the marmalade is melted and smooth, stirring occasionally.

6 Let cool, then add to the orange sections and strips of zest and stir to mix. Taste the sauce and add sugar if needed, then chill until serving.

3 PREPARE THE FRUIT

1 Peel the pineapple and cut it into rings (see box, below). Peel the apples using the vegetable peeler. Force the apple corer into each apple, through the stem end down to the base, and push out the cylinder containing the core and seeds.

Corer removes apple core and seeds neatly

Steady hand on work surface while coring apple

2 Cut the apples across into rings about ³/₈ inch thick.

ANNE SAYS
"If preparing ahead, sprinkle the apples with lemon juice to prevent discoloration."

3 Peel the bananas and cut them diagonally into 1-inch slices.

HOW TO PEEL PINEAPPLE AND CUT IT INTO RINGS

1 With a chef's knife, cut off the plume and base of the pineapple and set it upright, base-end down, on a chopping board. Cut away the peel in strips, working from top to bottom following the curve of the fruit and cutting deeply enough to remove the eyes with the pineapple skin.

Cut downward and deep enough to remove all peel

2 Cut the pineapple across into ¹/₂-inch-thick slices.

3 With a round cookie cutter, cut the core out of each slice.

4 DEEP-FRY THE FRITTERS

Add sugar while still whisking

1 If necessary, thin the batter with a little more beer to the consistency of thin cream. Whisk the egg whites until stiff peaks form. Sprinkle in the granulated sugar and continue whisking until glossy, 30 seconds.

2 Add the egg whites to the batter and fold them together: Cut down into the center of the bowl with the large metal spoon, scoop under the contents, and turn them over in a rolling motion. At the same time, with your other hand, turn the bowl counter-clockwise. Continue folding until the egg whites are thoroughly incorporated.

3 Heat the oil in the deep-fat fryer to 375° F. Heat the oven to very low, for keeping the fritters warm.

ANNE SAYS
"To test the oil temperature without a thermometer, drop in a cube of bread: It should turn golden brown in 40 seconds."

Apple rings should have thin coating of batter

Fry only a few pieces at a time

4 Dip 4-5 apple rings in the batter so they are completely covered. With the 2-pronged fork, lift out one ring at a time and drain 1-2 seconds so excess batter drips into the bowl. Lower the ring gently into the hot oil, then add a few more rings, one at a time.

! TAKE CARE !
It is important to deep-fry in small batches so the fryer is not crowded and the oil temperature remains constant.

Lift fritters from fat with slotted spoon, tilting to pour off excess fat

5 Fry the fritters until crisp and brown on one side, 2-3 minutes, then turn with the slotted spoon and brown the other side.

6 Transfer the fritters to the baking sheet lined with several layers of paper towels. Keep warm in the oven with the door propped open. Dip and deep-fry the remaining apple, pineapple and banana in the same way.

¡Ⓞ¡ TO SERVE

As soon as all the fritters have been fried, arrange them on a serving platter, sprinkle with the confectioners' sugar, and serve. Pass the fresh orange sauce separately.

Fritters have crisp beer-batter coating

Pineapple tops make a pretty decoration

V A R I A T I O N

FRUIT FRITTERS IN CHAMPAGNE BATTER WITH RASPBERRY COULIS

Champagne or any sparkling white wine replaces beer in these light fruit fritters, with a tangy raspberry coulis as an accompaniment.

1 Make the batter as directed, replacing the beer with an equal quantity of Champagne or sparkling white wine.

2 Omit the fresh orange sauce and make a raspberry coulis: Pick over 1 pint fresh or drained, defrosted raspberries, then purée them in a food processor or blender. Stir in 1-2 tbsp kirsch, if you like, and add 2-3 tbsp confectioners' sugar to taste. Work the purée through a strainer to remove the seeds and ensure the coulis is smooth.

3 Prepare the fruit as directed.

4 Deep-fry the fritters and serve with the raspberry coulis.

CARIBBEAN FLAMBEED PINEAPPLE

🍽 SERVES 6 🥣 WORK TIME 15-20 MINUTES* ♨ COOKING TIME 10-15 MINUTES

EQUIPMENT

2 cake pans

chef's knife

metal spatula

large metal spoon

ice-cream scoop

small round
cookie cutter**

large frying pan

bowls

wooden spoon

chopping board

** small knife can also be used

Rings of fresh pineapple are sautéed with brown sugar and pecans, flamed with dark rum, and topped with shredded coconut. Vanilla ice cream is a cooling accompaniment. When choosing a pineapple, give a quick tug to the plume – when ripe, the leaves should detach easily and the fruit should have a sweet odor. If you are short of time, storebought ice cream can replace the homemade vanilla ice cream (recipe on page 60).

GETTING AHEAD

The ice cream can be made up to 2 weeks ahead and kept in the freezer. The fruit can be prepared up to 4 hours ahead, then flambéed just before serving.

plus time for homemade ice cream

SHOPPING LIST

1	pineapple, weighing about 2 lb
½ cup	pecan halves
⅓ cup	unsweetened shredded coconut
½ cup	unsalted butter
½ cup	brown sugar
⅓ cup	dark rum
	vanilla ice cream for serving

INGREDIENTS

pineapple

vanilla
ice cream

unsweetened
shredded
coconut

pecan halves

brown sugar

unsalted butter

dark rum

ANNE SAYS

"If you are making your own ice cream, it will be very firm if made in advance, so let it soften in the refrigerator 30 minutes before serving."

ORDER OF WORK

1 PREPARE THE
  INGREDIENTS

2 FLAMBE THE
  PINEAPPLE

3 SERVE THE DISH

1 PREPARE THE INGREDIENTS

1 Heat the oven to 375° F. Cut the plume and base from the pineapple, then peel it, working from top to bottom following the curve of the fruit.

Use chef's knife to cut peel from pineapple

2 Cut the pineapple across into 12 thin slices and remove the cores with the cookie cutter.

Nuts are crisper when toasted

3 Put the pecans in one cake pan and the coconut in the other, spreading them both evenly.

4 Toast the pecans and coconut in the oven until golden, about 5 minutes, stirring occasionally with the wooden spoon so that they brown evenly. Let cool.

2 FLAMBE THE PINEAPPLE

1 Heat the butter in the frying pan until melted. Add the brown sugar.

Heat butter gently so it does not brown

Add brown sugar once butter has melted

2 Cook over low heat, stirring with the metal spoon, until the brown sugar has melted, about 2 minutes.

3 Add the pineapple rings and cook until tender, 3-5 minutes, turning them once.

Turn pineapple rings with metal spatula

ANNE SAYS
"*The pineapple rings should lie flat in the pan so, if necessary, cook the rings in batches.*"

5 Turn the heat to medium high. Add the rum to the pan and bring the liquid to a boil.

Pour rum into simmering butter-and-sugar mixture

4 Sprinkle the toasted pecan halves on top of the pineapple rings.

Scatter nuts evenly in pan

6 Hold a lighted match to the side of the pan to set the rum alight. Baste the fruit with the sauce until the flames subside, 2-3 minutes.

! TAKE CARE !
Flames can rise quite high, so stand back and keep hair and face away from the flames. Use a long-handled metal spoon for basting.

3 SERVE THE DISH

1 Transfer 2 rings of pineapple to each serving plate and add a scoop of vanilla ice cream. Spoon the rum-and-pecan sauce over the pineapple. Sprinkle with the toasted coconut and serve immediately.

Fresh pineapple rings have a glaze of butter, brown sugar, and rum

Vanilla ice cream gives a cool and creamy touch

V A R I A T I O N

CHERRIES JUBILEE

Cherries Jubilee were created to commemorate Queen Victoria's golden jubilee.

1 Pit 1 lb Bing or other dark sweet cherries.
2 Cook the cherries in the butter and brown sugar, omitting the pecans and coconut, and use ⅓ cup kirsch to flambé the cherries.
3 Put the cherries in 6 shallow bowls and top each with a scoop of vanilla ice cream. Spoon over the sauce and serve immediately.

V A R I A T I O N

FLAMBEED BANANAS FOSTER

This is a New Orleans dish, named after a local personality of the 1950s. Sugar-glazed almonds add texture and crunch to the softness of the bananas. Choose ripe bananas; their skins may have black spots, but there should be no large black patches.

1 Heat ¼ cup dark raisins with ½ cup water in a small saucepan, until very warm. Remove from the heat, cover, and let soak 15 minutes until plump. Drain them and discard the liquid.
2 To make sugar-glazed almonds for the topping, melt 1 tbsp unsalted butter in a small frying pan and stir in 1 tbsp granulated sugar. Add ⅓ cup sliced almonds and cook gently, stirring occasionally, until the nuts are coated and browned, 2-3 minutes. Remove from the heat and sprinkle with 1 tbsp more granulated sugar.
3 Peel 6 large ripe bananas and cut them crosswise in half. Cut each half lengthwise into 3-4 slices.
4 Cook the bananas in the butter and brown sugar as directed in the main recipe, sprinkling with ½ tsp ground cinnamon and the plumped raisins in place of the pecan halves. When the bananas are tender, pour in the dark rum and flambé.
5 Serve as directed, sprinkling the sugar-glazed almonds over each serving in place of the toasted coconut.

GRATIN OF FRESH BERRIES WITH SABAYON

¡©! SERVES 4   🥄 WORK TIME 15-20 MINUTES   🍲 BROILING TIME 1-2 MINUTES

EQUIPMENT

4 individual gratin dishes*

small knife

grater

whisk

large saucepan

large metal spoon

bowls**

plate

baking sheet

INGREDIENTS

mixed berries

egg yolks

lemon

Grand Marnier***

sugar

***Marsala can also be used

ANNE SAYS
"Look for berries in season to achieve the full fruity fragrance of this sumptuous dessert."

In this dessert, a selection of fresh berries is topped with fluffy sabayon sauce flavored with Grand Marnier or rich Marsala. Served in individual dishes, each gratin is broiled close to the heat to warm the fruit and give the sabayon an attractive golden-brown top. Professional chefs often save time by using a small blowtorch instead of the broiler. Choose ripe berries that are plump and full of color.

GETTING AHEAD

The berries can be prepared, arranged in the dishes, and refrigerated 4 hours ahead. Sabayon sauce separates on standing, so it must be made and the gratin broiled at the last minute.

ORDER OF WORK

1 PREPARE THE BERRIES

2 MAKE THE SABAYON

3 BROIL THE GRATIN

SHOPPING LIST

12 oz	mixed berries such as raspberries, strawberries, blackberries, loganberries, blueberries
1	lemon
3	egg yolks
1/4 cup	sugar
6 tbsp	Grand Marnier

*heatproof dessert plates can also be used

**to include 1 large heatproof bowl

1 PREPARE THE BERRIES

1 Pick over the berries, washing them only if they are dirty. Hull the strawberries. Cut any large berries in half or into quarters.

Arrange berries attractively in individual dishes

2 Divide the berries evenly among the gratin dishes, arranging them decoratively, and chill in the refrigerator.

2 MAKE THE SABAYON

Combine ingredients in heatproof bowl to whisk over hot water later

1 Heat the broiler. Grate the zest from half of the lemon.

ANNE SAYS
"Tap the grater firmly on the work surface to dislodge all the zest."

2 Put the egg yolks, sugar, and Grand Marnier in a large heatproof bowl and whisk them to mix.

3 Set the bowl over the saucepan half-filled with hot but not simmering water and start to whisk.

! TAKE CARE !
Make sure the bowl is large enough to sit in the saucepan without touching the water or the sauce will overheat and may curdle.

4 Continue whisking until the mixture is frothy and thick enough to leave a ribbon trail, 5-8 minutes. Take the sauce from the pan of hot water, whisk in the zest, and continue whisking 1-2 minutes until slightly cooled.

Mixture will become quite pale as it is whisked

3 BROIL THE GRATIN

Berries are warm and succulent

1 Arrange the gratin dishes on the baking sheet and spoon the sabayon over and around the berries. Broil about 6 inches from the heat until the sabayon is golden brown and the fruit is warm, 1-2 minutes.

🍴 **TO SERVE**
Transfer the hot dishes to plates for easy service and serve immediately.

Sabayon is broiled to deep golden brown

VARIATION
BERRIES AND ICE CREAM WITH SABAYON

1 Prepare the berries as directed.
2 Chill a large heatproof serving dish.
3 Take scoops from 1 quart of vanilla ice cream and pile them in the dish.
4 Arrange the berries decoratively on top of the ice cream. Chill.

5 Peel the zest from the lemon with a vegetable peeler, instead of grating it, and cut it into thin strips.
6 Make the sabayon and spoon it over the fruit. Broil as directed and serve immediately. Serves 6-8.

HOW TO SEED GRAPES

Many varieties of seedless grapes are now available, but if you have grapes with seeds, here are 2 ways to remove them.

To seed with a paper clip: Open a paper clip; insert the narrow end of the clip at the stem end of the grape. Twist the clip and remove to poke out the seeds.

To seed with a knife: Halve the grapes, then flick out the seeds with the tip of a small knife.

VARIATION
GRATIN OF CITRUS FRUIT AND GRAPES WITH SABAYON

This is a year-round variation of Gratin of Fresh Berries with Sabayon. The grapes should be firm and smooth.

1 Replace the berries with 4 medium navel oranges, 2 small grapefruit, and 3 oz green or black grapes.
2 Cut away the skin and white pith from the citrus fruits, following the curve of the fruit. Cut out the sections, cutting down both sides of the dividing membrane. Drain the sections on paper towels.
3 Stem the grapes and seed them if necessary (see box, left).
4 Arrange the citrus sections in a flower-petal design in heatproof dessert dishes, with the grapes in a ring around the outside.
5 Make the sabayon sauce, omitting the lemon zest. Broil the gratins as directed.

PEACH PIE

EQUIPMENT

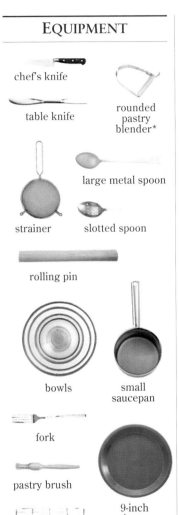

chef's knife

table knife

rounded pastry blender*

large metal spoon

strainer

slotted spoon

rolling pin

bowls

small saucepan

fork

pastry brush

wire rack

small knife

baking sheet

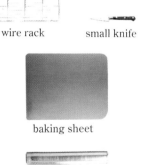

plastic wrap

*2 round-bladed knives can also be used

This is a real classic – ripe fresh peaches, their juice lightly thickened with flour and enclosed in a pastry lattice. When served "à la mode" with homemade vanilla ice cream, peach pie is the perfect summer dessert. Choose peaches that are ripe and full of juice, with no green tinge.

GETTING AHEAD

The pie can be made 1-2 days in advance and kept, covered, at room temperature, but it is best on the day it is baked.

* plus 45 minutes chilling time

SHOPPING LIST

For the pastry dough	
2 cups	flour
½ tsp	salt
½ cup	vegetable shortening
⅓ cup	unsalted butter
3 tbsp	water, more if needed
For the filling	
4-5	fresh ripe peaches, total weight about 1 lb
¼ cup	flour
¾ cup	sugar, more if needed
	salt
1-2 tbsp	lemon juice (optional)
For the glaze	
1	egg
½ tsp	salt

INGREDIENTS

peaches

sugar

vegetable shortening

egg

unsalted butter

flour

lemon juice (optional)

ORDER OF WORK

1 **MAKE THE PASTRY DOUGH**

2 **LINE THE PIE PAN**

3 **PREPARE THE FILLING; BAKE THE PIE**

1 MAKE THE PASTRY DOUGH

1 Sift the flour and salt into a large bowl using the strainer or a flour sifter.

2 Add the shortening and butter and cut them into the flour with the pastry blender.

3 Continue cutting until the mixture forms coarse crumbs.

Pastry blender is ideal tool for mixing dough ingredients

4 Sprinkle with the water and continue blending with the pastry blender until the dough can be gathered up into a ball. If the dough is dry, add 1-2 tbsp more water. Knead lightly until mixed, about 30 seconds.

5 Shape the dough into a ball, wrap tightly, and chill until firm, about 30 minutes.

2 LINE THE PIE PAN

1 Heat the oven to 400° F. Heat the baking sheet in the oven. Lightly flour the work surface and roll out two-thirds of the dough about 2 inches larger than the pie pan.

Rolling pin avoids need to handle pastry

2 Roll the dough around the rolling pin and drape it over the pie pan.

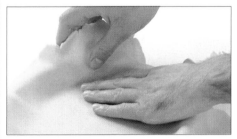

3 Lift the edges of the dough with one hand and press it well into the bottom of the pan with the other hand.

Reserve pastry trimmings to help make lattice

4 Using the table knife, trim off any excess dough even with the outer edge of the pan. Chill the pie shell 15 minutes.

3 PREPARE THE FILLING; BAKE THE PIE

Amount of sugar needed varies with ripeness of peaches

1 Immerse the peaches in boiling water and leave 10 seconds, then transfer to a bowl of cold water with the slotted spoon. Cut the peaches in half using the indentation on one side as a guide, remove the pit, and peel off the skin. Cut the peaches into ½-inch slices and put them in a large bowl.

2 Sprinkle the peaches with the flour, sugar, a pinch of salt, and lemon juice to help cut the sweetness, to taste.

3 Carefully stir the peaches until they are coated with the sugar mixture, then transfer them to the lined pie pan with the juices in the bowl.

4 Press any dough trimmings into the remaining dough and roll it out into a rectangle. Cut out 8 strips ½ inch wide; reserve the trimmings.

Lay strips over filling without stretching them

5 Lay half of the strips from left to right across the pie about ¾ inch apart. Fold back every other strip halfway and place a fifth strip over the unfolded strips across the center of the pie.

Arranging strips in this way gives lattice interwoven effect

6 Lay back the folded strips and fold back the alternates. Place the next strip about ¾ inch from the fifth. Continue until the pie is latticed. Turn the pie and repeat with the other half of the pie.

7 To make the glaze, in a small bowl, use the fork to beat the egg lightly with the salt. Trim the pastry strips even with the edge of the pie shell; reserve the trimmings. Moisten the ends of the strips with glaze and pinch with your fingers to seal them to the edge. Brush the lattice with glaze.

HOW TO MAKE PASTRY LEAVES

Pep up your presentation with a leafy border. Pastry leaves are very simple – and quick – to make.

Cut the dough into strips 1 inch wide, then cut diagonally across to make leaves. Mark veins on the leaves with the back of a knife. Curve the leaves with your fingers.

Overlap leaves slightly so they look natural

8 Re-roll the pastry trimmings and cut out leaves (see box, above). Lay the pastry leaves around the edge of the pie to cover the lattice ends.

🍽 **TO SERVE**
Serve individual pie portions warm or at room temperature.

9 Brush the leaves with glaze. Bake the pie in the oven on the heated baking sheet until the pastry is golden brown and the peaches are soft and bubbling, 40-45 minutes. Transfer the pie to the rack to cool slightly.

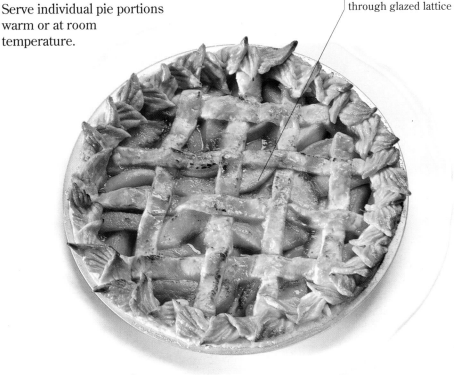

Golden peaches peep through glazed lattice

CHERRY PIE

This most famous of all American pies is made just like Peach Pie.

1 Pit 1 lb tart cherries.
2 Prepare the pie dough and line the pie pan as directed.
3 Stir the pitted cherries with 1 cup sugar, more if needed to taste, 1/3 cup flour, and 1/4 tsp almond extract, if you like. Transfer the coated cherries to the lined pie pan.

4 Cut the pastry strips, using a fluted ravioli cutter, and use to make a lattice as directed in the main recipe. Cut 2 more strips with the ravioli cutter and lay them around the edge of the pie to cover lattice ends.

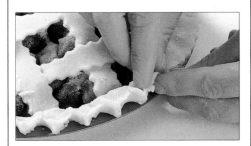

5 Flute the edge, pinching it with your fingers, and brush with glaze.
6 Bake the pie as directed. Serve at room temperature or slightly chilled.

NORMANDY PEAR TART
Tarte aux Poires Normande

 SERVES 6-8   WORK TIME 40-45 MINUTES WORK BAKING TIME 40-45 MINUTES

EQUIPMENT

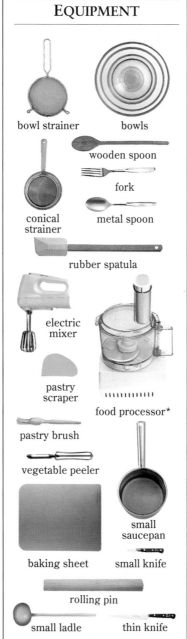

bowl strainer

bowls

wooden spoon

fork

conical strainer

metal spoon

rubber spatula

electric mixer

pastry scraper

food processor*

pastry brush

vegetable peeler

small saucepan

baking sheet

small knife

rolling pin

small ladle

thin knife

metal spatula

melon baller

9-inch loose-based tart pan

* blender or rotary cheese grater can also be used

This delicious tart has become a signature recipe of Normandy. Sliced pears are arranged like petals and baked in almond cream. Pears should be ripe, or they will discolor during cooking.

— GETTING AHEAD —
The tart is best eaten the day of baking, although it can be kept up to 2 days in an airtight container.

SHOPPING LIST

1	lemon
3-4	ripe medium pears, total weight about 1¹/₄ lb
	For the sweet pastry dough
1¹/₂ cups	flour
3	egg yolks
¹/₃ cup	sugar
	salt
¹/₃ cup	unsalted butter, more for pan
¹/₂ tsp	vanilla extract
	For the almond cream
³/₄ cup	whole blanched almonds
¹/₂ cup	unsalted butter, at room temperature
¹/₂ cup	sugar
1	egg
1	egg yolk
1 tbsp	kirsch
2 tbsp	flour
	For the apricot jam glaze
²/₃ cup	apricot jam
2-3 tbsp	kirsch or water

INGREDIENTS

pears

egg yolks

sugar

egg

lemon

apricot jam

unsalted butter

kirsch

whole blanched almonds

flour

vanilla extract

ORDER OF WORK

1. **MAKE THE SWEET PASTRY DOUGH**

2. **LINE THE TART PAN**

3. **MAKE THE ALMOND CREAM**

4. **PREPARE THE PEARS**

5. **ASSEMBLE AND BAKE THE TART**

1 MAKE THE SWEET PASTRY DOUGH

Pastry scraper is ideal tool for mixing dough

1 Sift the flour onto a work surface. Make a well in the center and add the egg yolks, sugar, and a pinch of salt. Using the rolling pin, pound the butter to soften it. Add the butter to the well with the vanilla extract.

2 Using your fingertips, work the ingredients in the well until thoroughly mixed.

3 Draw in the flour with the pastry scraper. With your fingers, work the flour into the other ingredients until coarse crumbs form. If they seem dry, add a little water.

5 Gather up the dough with the pastry scraper and continue to blend until it peels away from the work surface in one piece, 1-2 minutes. Shape into a ball, wrap tightly, and chill until firm, about 30 minutes.

! TAKE CARE !
Pastry doughs made with so much sugar are particularly delicate. Be sure to give the dough enough time to chill.

4 Press the dough into a ball. Lightly flour the work surface, then blend the dough by pushing it away from you with the heel of your hand.

2 LINE THE TART PAN

1 Brush the inside of the tart pan with melted butter. Unwrap the chilled pastry dough, then lightly flour the work surface and roll out the chilled dough to a round 2 inches larger than the tart pan.

Check size of rolled-out dough by placing tart pan on top

2 Roll up the dough around the rolling pin, then unroll it loosely over the tart pan.

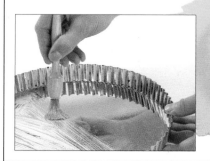

Drape dough over pan without stretching it

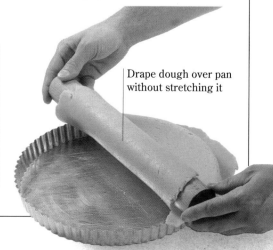

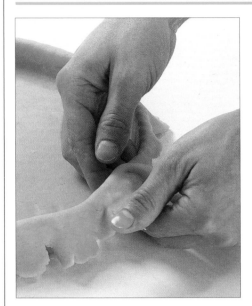

5 With both forefingers and thumbs, pinch the dough above the side of the tart pan to form a fluted edge. Prick the bottom of the tart shell with the fork to prevent air bubbles from forming during cooking. Chill the shell until firm, at least 15 minutes. Meanwhile, make the almond cream and prepare the pears.

Pinch to make neat fluted edge

3 Lift the edge of the dough with one hand and press it well into the bottom of the pan with the other hand. Leave a ridge of dough just inside the edge of the pan.

ANNE SAYS
"This ridge is pushed up over the edge of the pan to make a deep shell."

4 Roll the rolling pin over the top of the pan, pressing down lightly on the rolling pin to cut off the excess pastry dough. With your thumb, press the dough evenly up the side of the tart pan and above the top edge of the pan. Neaten the edge of the dough.

3 MAKE THE ALMOND CREAM

Sprinkle sugar into softened butter

1 Grind the almonds in 2-3 batches in the food processor.

! TAKE CARE !
Do not overwork the nuts or their oil will be released, creating a paste.

2 With the electric mixer or wooden spoon, cream the butter. Add the sugar and continue beating until fluffy and light, 2-3 minutes.

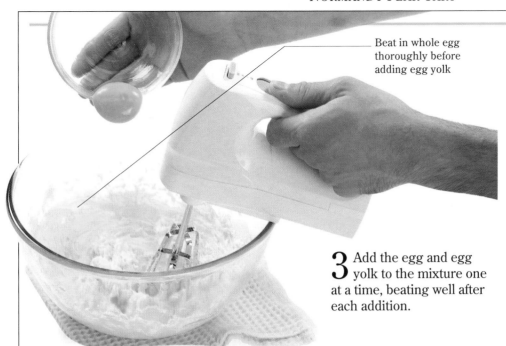

Beat in whole egg
thoroughly before
adding egg yolk

3 Add the egg and egg
yolk to the mixture one
at a time, beating well after
each addition.

4 Add the kirsch, then stir in the
ground almonds and flour.

4 ▸ PREPARE THE PEARS

1 Cut the lemon in half. Peel the
pears with the vegetable peeler. As
each pear is peeled, rub it all over with
the cut lemon to prevent it from
discoloring.

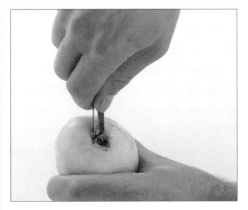

2 Twist the stem of each pear to
remove it and scoop out the flower
end with the tip of the peeler.

Melon baller
cuts out core
leaving neat
hollow

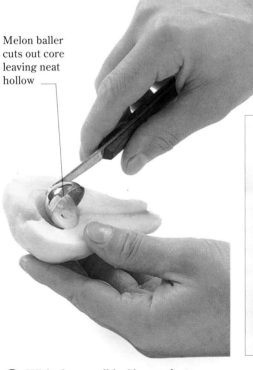

3 With the small knife cut the pears
lengthwise in half. Neatly remove
the core from the center of each pear
half with the melon baller or the tip of
the vegetable peeler. Rub all the cut
surfaces of each pear half with the cut
lemon again.

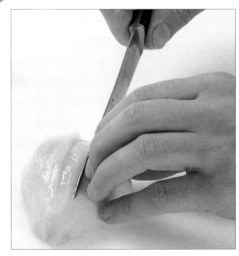

4 Set a pear half cut-side down on
a chopping board. Using the
thin-bladed knife, cut it lengthwise
into thin slices, leaving them joined
at the stem end. Repeat for 6 more of
the pear halves. Cut the last pear half
crosswise into thin slices.

ANNE SAYS
*"Each of the 7 fruit halves should hold
together neatly after slicing."*

HOW TO MAKE A FRUIT JAM OR JELLY GLAZE

A jam or jelly glaze is brushed on fruit to make it glisten and keep it moist. Make a red-currant jelly glaze to spread on red fruit; for other fruit, use apricot jam. A glaze can also be used to coat pastry so that the filling does not make the pastry soggy.

1 Melt the jam or jelly with the water or other liquid in a small saucepan, stirring occasionally with a wooden spoon.

2 Work jam glaze through a strainer. Return to the pan and melt again over low heat.

ANNE SAYS
"If using a jelly it will be smooth and need not be strained."

5 ASSEMBLE AND BAKE THE TART

1 Heat the oven to 400° F. Heat the baking sheet near the bottom of the oven. Spoon the almond cream into the chilled pastry shell and spread it evenly with the metal spatula.

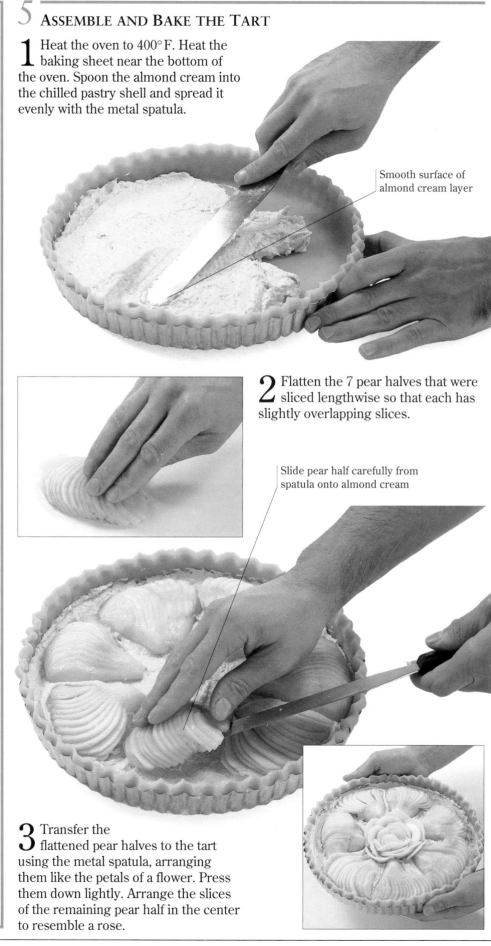

Smooth surface of almond cream layer

2 Flatten the 7 pear halves that were sliced lengthwise so that each has slightly overlapping slices.

Slide pear half carefully from spatula onto almond cream

3 Transfer the flattened pear halves to the tart using the metal spatula, arranging them like the petals of a flower. Press them down lightly. Arrange the slices of the remaining pear half in the center to resemble a rose.

Setting pan on hot baking sheet ensures that base of tart cooks thoroughly

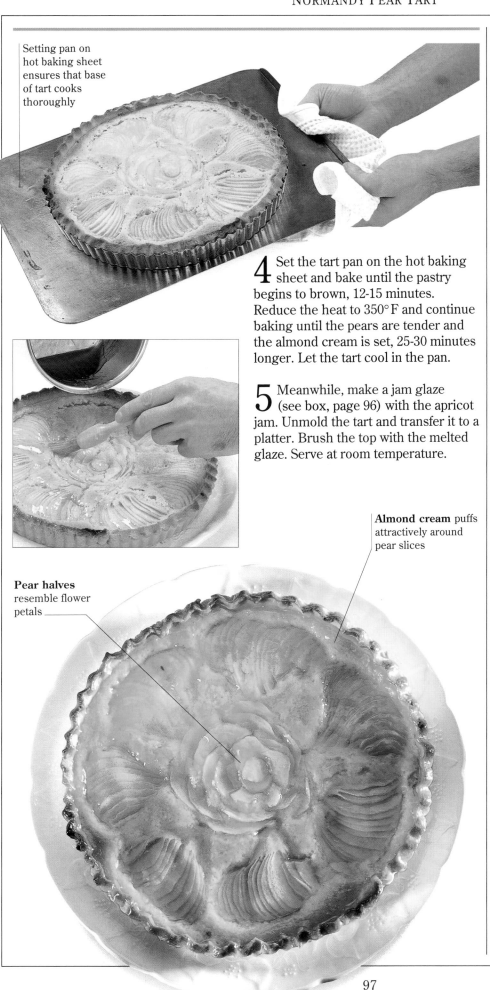

4 Set the tart pan on the hot baking sheet and bake until the pastry begins to brown, 12-15 minutes. Reduce the heat to 350°F and continue baking until the pears are tender and the almond cream is set, 25-30 minutes longer. Let the tart cool in the pan.

5 Meanwhile, make a jam glaze (see box, page 96) with the apricot jam. Unmold the tart and transfer it to a platter. Brush the top with the melted glaze. Serve at room temperature.

Almond cream puffs attractively around pear slices

Pear halves resemble flower petals

VARIATION

NORMANDY PEACH TART

Fresh, juicy peaches are used instead of ripe pears, as the basis for this version of Normandy Pear Tart.

1 Make the sweet pastry dough and line the tart pan as directed in the main recipe. Make the almond cream.
2 Immerse 2 lb peaches in a pan of boiling water, leave 10 seconds, then transfer to a bowl of cold water. Cut each peach in half, remove the pit, and peel off the skin. Cut each half into thin slices and flatten them as for the pears, forming ovals.
3 Arrange the peach ovals on the almond cream.
4 Bake the tart as directed, and brush with the apricot jam glaze.

PHYLLO APRICOT TURNOVERS

EQUIPMENT

saucepans

grater

small knife

chef's knife

pastry brush

metal spatula

plate

wire rack

strainer

wooden spoon

chopping board

bowl

dish towels

baking sheets

Phyllo is a multi-purpose dough, and not nearly as hard to work with as you might think. Here, phyllo is folded into triangles to enclose a filling of fresh apricots cooked with a spicy blend of cinnamon, nutmeg, and cloves. These light and flaky turnovers can be eaten with a knife and fork or your fingers.

GETTING AHEAD

The phyllo turnovers can be prepared, wrapped securely, and kept in the refrigerator up to 2 days; they also freeze well. Bake them just before serving.

SHOPPING LIST

1 lb	apricots
1	lemon
1 cup	sugar
1 tsp	ground cinnamon
	ground nutmeg
	ground cloves
2 tbsp	water
1-lb	package phyllo dough
¾ cup	unsalted butter

INGREDIENTS

apricots

unsalted butter

lemon

phyllo dough

ground nutmeg

ground cinnamon

ground cloves

sugar

! TAKE CARE !

Do not allow phyllo to dry out or it will be impossible to fold. Work with one sheet at a time, keeping the rest covered with a moistened dish towel.

ORDER OF WORK

1 MAKE THE APRICOT FILLING

2 FILL AND SHAPE THE PHYLLO TURNOVERS

3 BAKE THE PHYLLO TURNOVERS

1 MAKE THE APRICOT FILLING

Use small knife to slice apricot halves

1 Cut each apricot in half around the pit. Using both hands, give a quick, sharp twist to each half to loosen it from the pit. Scoop out the pit with the knife and discard. Cut each half into 4-5 pieces. Grate the zest from half of the lemon onto the plate.

2 In a medium saucepan, combine the apricots, lemon zest, three-quarters of the sugar, the cinnamon, and a pinch each of nutmeg and cloves. Add the water.

3 Cook gently, stirring occasionally, until the mixture thickens to the consistency of jam, 20-25 minutes. Transfer to the bowl and let cool.

ANNE SAYS
"Some apricots should stay in pieces to give the filling texture."

2 FILL AND SHAPE THE PHYLLO TURNOVERS

1 Heat the oven to 400° F. Lay a dish towel on the work surface and sprinkle it lightly with water.

2 Unroll the phyllo dough sheets on the towel and cut them lengthwise in half. Cover them with a second moistened towel.

Fold phyllo carefully to avoid wrinkles and splitting

3 Melt the butter in a small pan. Take one half sheet of dough from the pile and set it lengthwise on the work surface. Lightly brush half of the sheet lengthwise with butter and fold the other half on top.

Center apricot filling
on dough strip

4 Brush the strip of dough with more butter. Spoon 1-2 tsp of the cooled apricot filling onto the strip of dough about 1 inch from one end.

! TAKE CARE !
Do not put too much apricot filling in the turnovers or they will burst during cooking.

5 Fold a corner of the dough strip over the filling to meet the other edge of dough, forming a triangle.

6 Continue folding the strip over and over to form a triangle with the filling inside. Set the triangle on a baking sheet with the final edge underneath, and cover the baking sheet with a moistened dish towel.

ANNE SAYS
"Close the corners tightly so the filling does not leak."

Shape triangle gently
without squeezing it

7 Continue making triangles with the remaining phyllo dough and filling, arranging them on the baking sheets and keeping them covered with moistened dish towels.

3 BAKE THE PHYLLO TURNOVERS

1 Brush the top of each triangle with butter and sprinkle with the remaining sugar. Bake in the heated oven until golden brown and flaky, 12-15 minutes. With the metal spatula, transfer the turnovers to the rack to cool slightly, and serve warm or at room temperature.

Sugar glaze gives crisp finish

Phyllo pastry is flaky and delicate

V A R I A T I O N

PHYLLO BERRY TURNOVERS

Mixed red berries replace the fresh apricots in Phyllo Apricot Turnovers.

1 Hull 1½ cups strawberries and pick over ¾ cup raspberries. Cut strawberries in half or into quarters, according to size. Put all the fruit in a bowl, sprinkle with ⅓ cup sugar and toss lightly to combine.
2 Fill each triangle with a scant 1 tbsp berries. Brush with butter, sprinkle with sugar, and bake as directed.
3 Decorate each serving with raspberries and mint sprigs, if you like.

V A R I A T I O N

PHYLLO APRICOT PURSES

An attractive alternative to pastry triangles, here squares of phyllo dough are wrapped up around the filling and the ends are lightly twisted to resemble a coin purse.

1 Make the apricot filling as directed.
2 Take 4 of the sheets of phyllo dough, keeping them in a stack. With a chef's knife, cut the layered sheets lengthwise, then crosswise to make 4½- to 5-inch squares. Discard any dough trimmings.
3 Keeping the remaining squares and uncut dough covered, place one square on the work surface and brush it with butter. Set a second square on top, at a 45° angle to the first, and butter it. Repeat to make a stack of 4 squares.
4 Spoon a scant 2 tsp cooled apricot filling into the center and pull the points of the squares up over the filling to make a purse. Twist it gently to seal the purse tightly.
5 Tie the purse closed with a small piece of string. Continue with the remaining stacks of squares, then repeat the process with the remaining sheets of dough and filling, to make 24 purses in all.
6 Bake as directed, then cut off the string. Serve on individual plates, with 3 warm apricot purses on each.

CARAMELIZED UPSIDE-DOWN APPLE TART

Tarte Tatin

 SERVES 8   WORK TIME 45-50 MINUTES   BAKING TIME 20-25 MINUTES

EQUIPMENT

chef's knife

small knife

heavy-based deep
frying pan or
skillet, with metal
handle (9-10 inch
diameter)

small plate

pastry
scraper

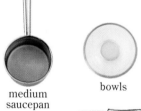
medium
saucepan

bowls

vegetable peeler

wooden spoon

large 2-pronged
fork

melon baller

chopping board

metal spatula

candy thermometer

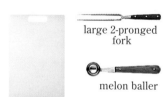
strainer

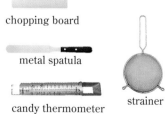
rolling pin

Tarte Tatin is named for two impoverished
gentlewomen, from the French region of Sologne,
who earned their living by baking and selling their
father's favorite apple tart. The secret of this
upside-down tart lies in cooking the apples in the
caramel itself, so it flavors deep inside the fruit. It
is delicious served warm with crème fraîche.

GETTING AHEAD

The tart can be baked 6-8 hours ahead and kept at room
temperature. Warm the tart briefly on top of the stove and
unmold it just before serving.

SHOPPING LIST

14–16	apples, total weight about 5 lb
1	lemon
½ cup	unsalted butter
1 cup	sugar
	crème fraîche for serving (see box, page 106)
For the pastry dough	
⅓ cup	unsalted butter
1½ cups	flour
2	egg yolks
1½ tbsp	sugar
	salt
1 tbsp	water, more if needed

INGREDIENTS

lemon

apples

unsalted
butter

flour

crème fraîche

egg yolks

sugar

ANNE SAYS

"*Crème fraîche is the ideal
accompaniment for the
caramel-steeped fruit tart. If
you are baking ahead, make
the crème fraîche at the same
time, because its flavor takes
6-8 hours to develop.*"

ORDER OF WORK

1 MAKE THE PASTRY
DOUGH

2 PREPARE AND
CARAMELIZE THE
APPLES

3 BAKE AND
UNMOLD THE TART

1 MAKE THE PASTRY DOUGH

Add other dough ingredients to well in flour

1 Using the rolling pin, pound the butter to soften it slightly. Sift the flour onto a work surface and make a well in the center. Put the egg yolks, sugar, and a pinch of salt in the center of the well, then add the softened butter and the water.

2 Using your fingertips, work the ingredients in the well until thoroughly mixed.

3 Draw the flour into the well using the pastry scraper. With your fingers, work the flour into the other ingredients until coarse crumbs form. If they seem dry, add a little more water. Press the dough into a ball.

Heel of hand only is used for blending dough

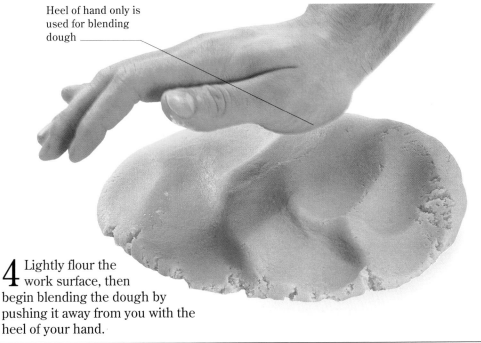

4 Lightly flour the work surface, then begin blending the dough by pushing it away from you with the heel of your hand.

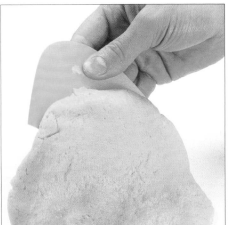

5 Gather up the dough with the pastry scraper and blend until it is very smooth and peels away from the work surface in one piece, 1-2 minutes. Shape into a ball, wrap it tightly, and chill until firm, about 30 minutes.

HOW TO HALVE AND CORE AN APPLE

If you use the correct technique and equipment for preparing fruit, no matter how simple these are, you are more likely to get a professional finish.

1 With the point of a small knife, cut around the stem end of the apple; remove the stem. Repeat with the flower end.

2 With the same knife, cut the apple lengthwise in half.

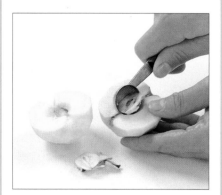

3 With a melon baller, carefully scoop out the core and seeds from the center of each apple half, leaving as neat a shape as possible.

2 PREPARE AND CARAMELIZE THE APPLES

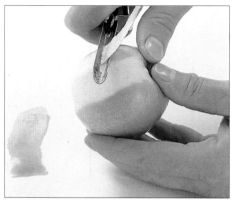

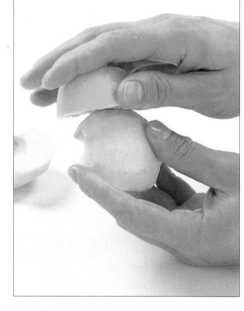

1 With the vegetable peeler or a small knife, carefully remove the outer peel from the apples in thin lengthwise strips. Halve and core the apples (see box, left).

2 Cut the lemon in half and rub the apples all over with the cut lemon to prevent discoloration.

Pour sugar into melted butter all at once

3 Melt the butter in the frying pan. Add the sugar.

When butter starts to sizzle, add sugar

4 Cook over medium heat, stirring occasionally with the wooden spoon, until caramelized to a deep golden brown, 3-5 minutes. Remove from the heat and let cool to tepid.

! TAKE CARE !
Cook gently once the caramel starts to color because it burns easily.

Arrange second circle of apple halves facing in opposite direction to first

Apple halves fit snugly into each other in pan

5 Arrange the apple halves upright in concentric circles to fill the pan. Prop up the first apple with the wooden spoon, then lean the others against it. The apples will shrink during cooking, so pack them tightly here.

6 Cook the apples over high heat until caramelized, 15-25 minutes. Turn once to caramelize on both sides.

ANNE SAYS
"Cooking time depends on the apples you use. When cooked they should be tender but still retain their shape, and very little juice should remain."

Use 2-pronged fork to turn apples carefully

7 When the apples are completely caramelized, take the pan from the heat and let cool 10-15 minutes. Heat the oven to 375°F.

3 BAKE AND UNMOLD THE TART

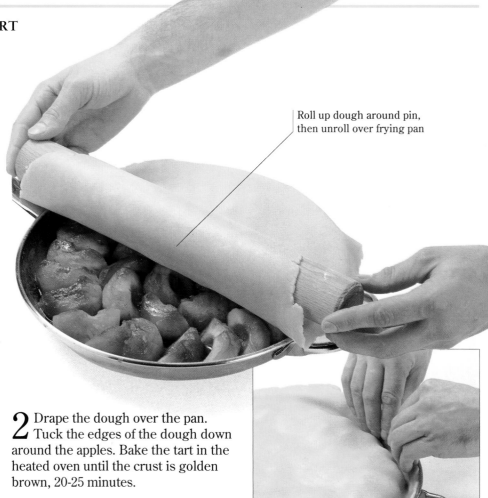

Roll up dough around pin, then unroll over frying pan

1 Roll out the pastry dough to a round about 1 inch larger than the frying pan. Roll up the dough around the rolling pin.

2 Drape the dough over the pan. Tuck the edges of the dough down around the apples. Bake the tart in the heated oven until the crust is golden brown, 20-25 minutes.

HOW TO MAKE CREME FRAICHE

When unpasteurized cream is left to stand, it develops a full, slightly sour taste. This is crème fraîche, the standard cream in France. Modern production methods use pasteurized cream that is recultured by adding bacteria to replace those destroyed by pasteurization. It can be purchased at some supermarkets, but if you find it difficult to obtain, it is easy to make with this recipe.

SHOPPING LIST

2 cups	heavy cream
1 cup	buttermilk or sour cream

1 Pour the heavy cream into a medium saucepan, add the buttermilk or sour cream, and stir to mix. Heat gently to 75° F. Pour the mixture into a glass measuring cup or a bowl.

2 Cover with a plate, leaving a gap for air. Leave at room temperature (70° F), until the mixture has thickened and tastes slightly acid, 6-8 hours. Stir, then cover and refrigerate.

3 Let the tart cool to tepid in the pan, then unmold it: Set a serving platter on top of the pan; holding firmly together, invert the two. If any apples stick to the pan, remove with a metal spatula and replace on the tart. Spoon some caramel from the platter over the apples. Serve with crème fraîche.

Lift pan away carefully so arrangement of apples is not disturbed

Caramel seeps through tart and forms a pool on plate

Apples are coated with caramel to give them a golden glow

V A R I A T I O N

CARAMELIZED UPSIDE-DOWN PEAR TART

Caramelized pears are just as delicious as apples in this variation of Tarte Tatin.

1 Peel, halve, and core 12-14 pears (total weight about 5 lb).

ANNE SAYS
"*Pears may produce more liquid than apples and so take longer to cook in the caramel until the liquid has evaporated.*"

2 Caramelize the pears as directed for the apples in the main recipe, arranging them on their sides in the pan with the tapered ends toward the center of the pan.
3 Cover with the pastry dough. Bake the tart and unmold as directed.

FRESH FRUIT TARTLETS

 SERVES 8   WORK TIME 40-45 MINUTES*   BAKING TIME 11-13 MINUTES

EQUIPMENT

saucepans, 1 with lid

fork

paper towels

bent metal spatula

8 4-inch tartlet molds

whisk

small knife

plastic wrap

pastry brush

strainer

slotted spoon

pastry scraper

small ladle

metal spoon

bowls

baking sheet   wire rack

aluminum foil

rolling pin

INGREDIENTS

mixed fresh fruit

vanilla extract

apricot jam**

egg yolks

unsalted butter

vanilla bean

sugar

milk

flour

**red-currant jelly is used if all fruit is red

A crisp, sweet pastry shell lined with vanilla pastry cream is the ideal way to display the best of fresh fruit. Finished with a jam glaze, contrasting colors, such as red raspberries, golden peaches, and green kiwi fruit, look especially good. All fruit will look attractive, though; choose whatever is in season.

*plus 1 hour chilling time

SHOPPING LIST

1 lb	mixed fresh fruit, such as kiwi fruit, raspberries, grapes, peaches
For the sweet pastry dough	
1½ cups	flour
4	egg yolks
7 tbsp	sugar
½ tsp	salt
½ tsp	vanilla extract
6 tbsp	unsalted butter, more for tartlet molds
For the vanilla pastry cream	
1½ cups	milk
1	vanilla bean or 2 tsp vanilla extract
5	egg yolks
⅓ cup	sugar
¼ cup	flour
1 tbsp	unsalted butter
For the jam glaze	
¾ cup	apricot jam or red-currant jelly
2-3 tbsp	water

ORDER OF WORK

1 **MAKE THE SWEET PASTRY DOUGH**

2 **MAKE THE PASTRY CREAM**

3 **LINE AND BLIND BAKE THE TARTLET SHELLS**

4 **PREPARE THE FRUIT AND GLAZE**

5 **ASSEMBLE THE TARTLETS**

1 MAKE THE SWEET PASTRY DOUGH

Side of well must be high enough to contain ingredients in center

1 Sift the flour onto a work surface and make a well in the center.

2 Put the egg yolks, sugar, salt, and vanilla extract in the well in the center of the sifted flour.

Softening butter makes it easy to blend with other ingredients

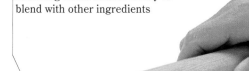

3 Using the rolling pin, pound the butter to soften it slightly and add it to the well.

4 With your fingertips, work the ingredients in the well until thoroughly mixed. Draw in the flour with the pastry scraper.

Work ingredients together before mixing in flour

5 With your fingers, work the flour into the other ingredients until coarse crumbs form. Press the dough into a ball.

6 Lightly flour the work surface, then blend the dough by pushing it away from you with the heel of your hand.

Gently knead dough just to mix it

7 Gather up the dough with the pastry scraper and blend until it is very smooth and peels away from the work surface in one piece, 1-2 minutes.

8 Shape the dough into a ball, wrap it tightly, and chill until firm, about 30 minutes.

! TAKE CARE !
Pastry doughs made with this quantity of sugar are particularly delicate. Be sure to give the dough enough time to chill.

2 MAKE THE PASTRY CREAM

1 Bring the milk to a boil in a saucepan with the split-open vanilla bean, if using. Remove the pan from the heat, cover, and let stand 10-15 minutes. In a bowl, whisk together the egg yolks, sugar, and flour just to mix.

Use large bowl to whisk mixture

Milk is flavored with vanilla bean

2 Whisk in the hot milk until thoroughly combined. Return the mixture to the pan and cook over low heat, whisking constantly, until the flour has cooked and the cream is thick, 2-3 minutes. Simmer the cream over low heat 2 minutes.

ANNE SAYS
"Simmering the pastry cream cooks the flour so it leaves no aftertaste."

3 Transfer the pastry cream to another bowl and remove the vanilla bean if using, or stir in the vanilla extract. Rub the butter over the surface of the cream to prevent a skin from forming. Let cool.

3 LINE AND BLIND BAKE THE TARTLET SHELLS

1 Brush each of the tartlet molds with melted butter.

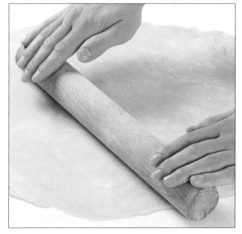

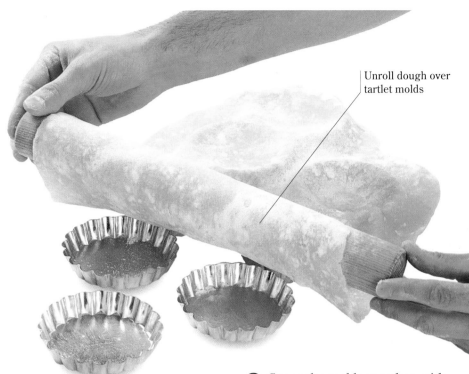

Unroll dough over tartlet molds

2 Lightly flour the work surface. Roll out the dough to ⅛ inch thickness.

3 Group the molds together, with their edges nearly touching. Roll the dough loosely around the rolling pin and drape it over the molds so all are covered.

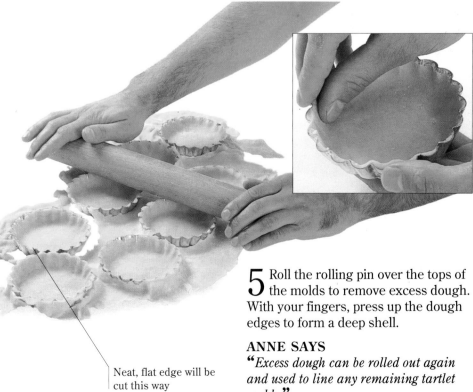

4 Tear off a small piece of dough from the edge, form it into a ball, dip it in flour, and use it to push the dough into the molds.

ANNE SAYS
"Brush off any excess flour from the dough."

Neat, flat edge will be cut this way

5 Roll the rolling pin over the tops of the molds to remove excess dough. With your fingers, press up the dough edges to form a deep shell.

ANNE SAYS
"Excess dough can be rolled out again and used to line any remaining tartlet molds."

6 Set the molds on the baking sheet and prick the dough with the fork to prevent it from puffing during cooking. Chill until firm, about 30 minutes. Heat the oven to 400°F.

Foil ensures that tartlet shell keeps its shape during baking

7 Line each tartlet shell with a piece of foil, pressing it down well.

ANNE SAYS
"Alternatively, omit the foil and line each tartlet shell with a mold of the same size, baking the dough in 2 batches."

8 Bake the shells in the heated oven until the pastry is set, 6-8 minutes. Remove the foil and continue baking until thoroughly cooked, about 5 minutes longer.

Handle tartlet shells with care so you do not damage them

9 With the spatula, transfer the tartlet molds to the wire rack to cool. When cold, remove each tartlet shell from its mold.

4 PREPARE THE FRUIT AND GLAZE

1 Peel the skin off the kiwi fruit in strips, working from top to bottom following the curve of the fruit. Slice the fruit, then cut the slices into quarters. Pick over raspberries.

ANNE SAYS
"If using strawberries, hull them and wash them only if they are dirty; cut any large berries in half. Peel and section tangerines, discarding any seeds."

2 Remove grapes from the stems, wash, and dry them. If the grapes are not seedless, remove the seeds with an opened paper clip (see box, page 87). Immerse peaches in a pan of boiling water, leave 10 seconds, then transfer with the slotted spoon to a bowl of cold water. Cut each peach in half, remove the pit, and peel off the skin. Cut the halves into slices.

3 Make the jam glaze, using apricot jam if the fruits are mixed in color, or red-currant jelly if they are all red fruit. Melt the jam or jelly with the water in a small saucepan. Work it through the strainer and melt again over low heat.

ANNE SAYS
"If using jelly, it will not need to be strained."

5 ASSEMBLE THE TARTLETS

1 Brush the inside of each tartlet shell with the melted jam glaze.

2 Half-fill each shell with the cooled pastry cream, smoothing the top with the back of the spoon.

Make decorative pattern with fruit

3 Arrange the fruit on top of the cream. Brush the fruit with the jam glaze.

Jam glaze makes fruit glisten like jewels

Green fruit contrasts with red and golden fruit

VARIATION

FRESH FRUIT TART

This full-size tart offers a striking presentation of fresh fruit arranged in concentric circles over vanilla pastry cream.

1 Make and chill the pastry dough as directed. Roll out the dough to ⅛-inch thickness and use to line a 10-inch tart pan. Prick the dough with a fork to prevent it from puffing during cooking. Chill until firm, about 30 minutes.

2 Line the tart shell with a double thickness of foil, pressing it well into the bottom edge. Half-fill the foil with dry beans or rice to weigh down the dough. Bake as directed, allowing about 15 minutes with the foil and beans; remove the foil and and beans and bake 7-10 minutes longer.

3 Make the pastry cream, and prepare a selection of fresh fruit and a jam glaze as directed.

4 Brush the tart shell with glaze, add the pastry cream, and top it with concentric rings of fruit. Glaze the fruit to finish.

GETTING AHEAD

The tartlet shells can be baked 2 days in advance and stored in an airtight container. The pastry cream can be made 1 day ahead and refrigerated, tightly covered.

CHERRY STRUDEL

 SERVES 6-8   WORK TIME 45-50 MINUTES*   BAKING TIME 30-40 MINUTES

EQUIPMENT

metal spatula**

chef's knife

cherry pitter

small saucepan

whisk

pastry brush

grater

strainer

bowls

dish towel

chopping board

plate

bed sheet

baking sheet

metal skewer

rolling pin

**pastry scraper can also be used

INGREDIENTS

tart cherries   egg

light brown sugar   ground cinnamon   walnuts

lemon   granulated sugar

unsalted butter   brandy   heavy cream

confectioners' sugar   lemon juice

flour

Don't be intimidated by making the ultra-thin strudel pastry; the trick is to knead the dough thoroughly so it is elastic. You will, however, need a large work table and a sheet to cover it.

GETTING AHEAD

Because strudel dough dries out easily, the strudel should be assembled and cooked at once. It is best eaten the day of baking, but can be kept in the refrigerator up to 24 hours. If baked ahead, reheat in a 350°F oven, 10-15 minutes.

* plus 45 minutes resting time

SHOPPING LIST

1	lemon
1 lb	tart cherries
½ cup	walnuts
½ cup	light brown sugar
1 tsp	ground cinnamon
	confectioners' sugar to finish
	For the strudel dough
2 cups	flour, more if needed
1	egg
½ cup	water
½ tsp	lemon juice
	salt
½ cup	unsalted butter, more for baking sheet
	For the Chantilly cream
1 cup	heavy cream
2 tbsp	granulated sugar
2 tbsp	brandy or 1 tsp vanilla extract

ORDER OF WORK

1 MAKE THE STRUDEL DOUGH

2 PREPARE THE FILLING AND CHANTILLY CREAM

3 ROLL AND STRETCH THE STRUDEL DOUGH

4 FILL AND BAKE THE STRUDEL

1 MAKE THE STRUDEL DOUGH

1 Sift the flour onto the work surface and make a well in the center. In a bowl, beat the egg to mix with the water, lemon juice, and a pinch of salt and pour into the well.

2 Work the ingredients in the well, drawing in a little of the flour with your fingertips.

3 Gradually draw in the remaining flour with the metal spatula, continuing to work the flour in with your fingertips. Gently knead in just enough flour so that the dough forms a ball; it should be quite soft.

4 Flour the work surface and knead the dough 5-7 minutes, picking it up and throwing it down, until shiny and smooth. Shape into a ball, cover with a bowl, and let rest 30 minutes. Meanwhile, prepare the filling.

ANNE SAYS
"Thorough kneading is critical for creating an elastic dough. Alternatively, work the dough in an electric mixer with the dough hook."

Kneading dough thoroughly makes it elastic

Dough will "relax" while it sits and will be easier to stretch

2 PREPARE THE FILLING AND CHANTILLY CREAM

1 Pit all the cherries (see box, page 116). Grate the zest from the lemon onto the plate.

2 Using the chef's knife, coarsely chop the walnuts.

ANNE SAYS
"Nuts are best chopped by hand to control the finished texture, although this will always be uneven."

3 To make the Chantilly cream, pour the cream into a chilled bowl and whip until soft peaks form. Add the sugar and brandy or vanilla extract and continue whipping until the cream forms stiff peaks and the whisk leaves clear marks in the cream. Chill.

3 ROLL AND STRETCH THE STRUDEL DOUGH

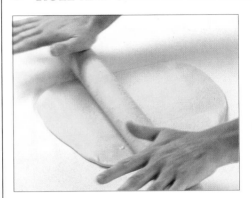

1 Cover the work table with the bed sheet and lightly flour it. Roll out the dough on the sheet to as large a square as possible. Cover it with the damp dish towel and let rest about 15 minutes. Heat the oven to 375° F, and butter the baking sheet. Melt the butter in the small saucepan.

HOW TO PIT CHERRIES

Choose firm cherries with shiny skin; avoid any with a dry stem.

To pit with a cherry pitter: This convenient tool pushes the pit through the fruit, leaving a full hollow. As a result, more of the cherry juices will be released when the cherries are cooked.

To pit with a vegetable peeler: Insert the tip of the peeler in the stem-end, rotate around the pit, and scoop it out. The result is neater than if a cherry pitter is used, and more of the juices will be retained.

Flour your hands from time to time while stretching dough

Any small holes that appear will not show when the dough is rolled up

2 Flour your hands and place them under the dough. Starting at the center and working outward, carefully stretch the dough with the backs of both hands. Continue to work outward as the dough gets thinner, gently lifting and flopping it on the surface. It should be as large a square as possible.

3 At once, brush the dough thoroughly with about three-quarters of the melted butter.

! TAKE CARE !

The stretched dough dries quickly and becomes brittle.

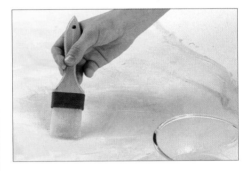

4 FILL AND BAKE THE STRUDEL

Sprinkle filling ingredients evenly over dough

1 Sprinkle the buttered strudel dough with the pitted cherries, chopped walnuts, brown sugar, lemon zest, and cinnamon. Trim the thick edge of the dough, pulling it out and pinching it off with your fingers.

DRIED FRUIT STRUDEL

When fresh cherries are not in season, try this dried fruit version of Cherry Strudel.

Use wide pastry brush to apply melted butter

2 Roll up the strudel with the help of the sheet. Transfer the roll to the prepared baking sheet and shape it into a crescent.

3 Brush the strudel with the remaining melted butter and bake in the heated oven until the skewer inserted in the center of the strudel for 30 seconds is hot when withdrawn, 30-40 minutes. The strudel should be crisp and golden brown.

1 Coarsely chop 1 lb mixed dried fruit (apricots, prunes, dates, raisins, figs), discarding any pits. Put the fruit in a small pan, cover with 1/2 cup dark rum and 1/2 cup water, and heat gently, stirring occasionally, about 5 minutes. Take from the heat and leave until the mixture has cooled and all the dried fruit is plump.
2 Meanwhile, make the Chantilly cream as directed, flavoring it with vanilla extract or rum.
3 Drain the fruits thoroughly, discarding the liquid.
4 Prepare and stretch the strudel dough as directed in the main recipe; brush with melted butter.
5 Sprinkle the dough with the dried fruit, chopped walnuts, brown sugar, and cinnamon; omit the lemon zest.
6 Roll and bake as directed. Serve with the Chantilly cream.

¡O¡ TO SERVE
Sprinkle the strudel with confectioners' sugar and serve hot or cold, with the Chantilly cream.

Fresh cherries add a pretty touch

Pastry is deliciously light and flaky

HAZELNUT TORTE WITH STRAWBERRIES

🍽 SERVES 8 🥣 WORK TIME 40-45 MINUTES* ☕ BAKING TIME 15-18 MINUTES

EQUIPMENT

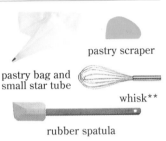

pastry scraper

pastry bag and small star tube

whisk**

rubber spatula

plastic wrap

chef's knife

bowl strainer

small ladle

small knife

metal spatula

conical strainer

dish towel

3 baking sheets

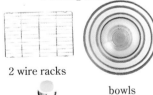

2 wire racks

bowls

food processor***

8-inch diameter saucepan lid

**electric mixer can also be used
***blender can also be used

An impressive three-layer castle of hazelnut pastry sandwiched with strawberries and whipped cream. A tart raspberry coulis is an ideal accompaniment.

GETTING AHEAD

The pastry rounds can be baked 1-2 days ahead and kept in an airtight container or can be frozen. The torte can be assembled up to 4 hours ahead and refrigerated.

*plus 30-60 minutes chilling time

SHOPPING LIST

1 quart	strawberries
	fresh mint sprigs for decoration
	For the hazelnut pastry
2 cups	hazelnuts
²/₃ cup	granulated sugar
1 cup	flour
¹/₂ tsp	salt
²/₃ cup	unsalted butter
1	egg yolk
	For the raspberry coulis
2 cups	fresh or drained defrosted raspberries
2-3 tbsp	confectioners' sugar
1-2 tbsp	kirsch (optional)
	For the Chantilly cream
1¹/₂ cups	heavy cream
1¹/₂ tbsp	granulated sugar
1 tsp	vanilla extract

INGREDIENTS

hazelnuts

strawberries

raspberries

confectioners' sugar

egg yolk

fresh mint

unsalted butter

heavy cream

flour

vanilla extract

kirsch (optional)

granulated sugar

ORDER OF WORK

1 MAKE THE HAZELNUT PASTRY DOUGH

2 SHAPE AND BAKE THE HAZELNUT PASTRY LAYERS

3 MAKE THE COULIS AND CHANTILLY CREAM; ASSEMBLE TORTE

1 MAKE THE HAZELNUT PASTRY DOUGH

Use rough-textured towel to rub skins from nuts

1 Heat the oven to 350° F. Spread the hazelnuts on the baking sheet. Toast until lightly browned, stirring occasionally so that the nuts color evenly, taking care that they do not burn, 8-10 minutes. While still hot, rub the nuts in the dish towel to remove the skins, then leave to cool.

2 In the food processor, grind the nuts with the granulated sugar to a fine powder.

ANNE SAYS
"If using a blender, grind the nuts and sugar in 2-3 batches."

Butter is cut into cubes to make it easy to work

Mix quickly – using your fingertips only – for a light result

3 Put the ground nut mixture on the work surface and sift the flour and salt on top. Make a well in the center of the ingredients and add the butter and egg yolk.

4 Using your fingertips, work the butter and egg yolk together in the well, drawing in a little of the ground nut and flour mixtures, until soft and thoroughly mixed.

5 Draw in the nut and flour mixture with the pastry scraper, working them into the butter mixture with your fingers until combined. Press the dough into a ball.

6 Sprinkle the work surface lightly with flour; place the dough on the work surface and blend the dough by pushing it away from you with the heel of your hand.

ANNE SAYS
"The dough will be quite sticky."

Dough is ready to chill

7 Gather up the dough with the pastry scraper and continue to blend gently until it is very smooth in texture.

8 Shape the dough into a ball, wrap it tightly, and chill until firm, at least 30 minutes.

! TAKE CARE !
Pastry doughs made with nuts are particularly delicate. Be sure to give the dough enough time to chill.

2 SHAPE AND BAKE THE HAZELNUT PASTRY LAYERS

Using heel of hand keeps dough from being worked too much and becoming soft

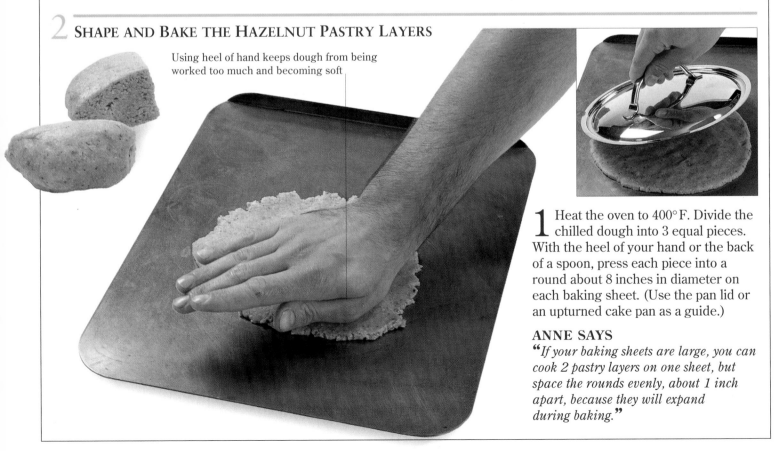

1 Heat the oven to 400° F. Divide the chilled dough into 3 equal pieces. With the heel of your hand or the back of a spoon, press each piece into a round about 8 inches in diameter on each baking sheet. (Use the pan lid or an upturned cake pan as a guide.)

ANNE SAYS
"If your baking sheets are large, you can cook 2 pastry layers on one sheet, but space the rounds evenly, about 1 inch apart, because they will expand during baking."

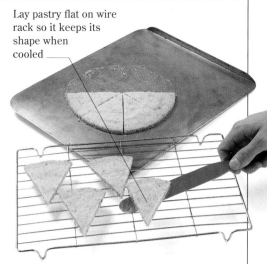

Lay pastry flat on wire rack so it keeps its shape when cooled

2 Bake the pastry layers in the heated oven until the edges begin to brown, 15-18 minutes. While they are still warm, trim them with the chef's knife to neat rounds using the pan lid as a guide.

! TAKE CARE !
Do not let the pastry cool before trimming or the rounds may break.

3 Using the chef's knife, cut one of the layers all the way across into 8 equal wedges. Let all the pastry layers and the wedges cool to tepid on the baking sheets.

4 Using the metal spatula, carefully transfer the pastry triangles and rounds from the baking sheets to the wire racks to cool completely.

ANNE SAYS
"If the rounds stick, warm them on the baking sheets in the oven, 2-3 minutes, to loosen them from the sheets."

3 MAKE THE COULIS AND CHANTILLY CREAM; ASSEMBLE TORTE

Point of small knife lifts out hulls

1 To make the raspberry coulis, pick over the berries, then purée them in the food processor. Stir in confectioners' sugar to taste, and the kirsch, if you like. Work the purée through the conical strainer to remove the seeds.

2 Hull the strawberries, washing them only if they are dirty. Set 8 small berries aside for decoration. Halve the remaining strawberries, or quarter them if they are large.

! TAKE CARE !
Washing softens strawberries, so only wash them if absolutely necessary.

3 To make the Chantilly cream, pour the cream into a chilled bowl and whip until soft peaks form. Add the sugar and vanilla extract and continue whipping until the cream forms stiff peaks and the whisk leaves clear marks in the cream. Spoon about one-quarter of the cream into the pastry bag.

4 Set one round of pastry on a serving plate. Cover with about one-quarter of the remaining Chantilly cream, and arrange half of the strawberries on top.

6 Set the second round of pastry on top and spread with half of the remaining Chantilly cream.

ANNE SAYS
"Slide the pastry round directly from the wire rack to avoid breaking it."

7 Cover with the remaining strawberries, spread the rest of the Chantilly cream on top and smooth.

5 Cover the strawberries with more Chantilly cream, spreading lightly with the rubber spatula.

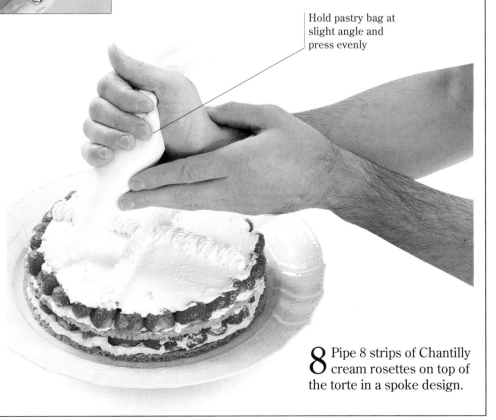

Use rubber spatula to spread cream lightly

Chantilly cream will help make second pastry round stick when placed on top

Hold pastry bag at slight angle and press evenly

8 Pipe 8 strips of Chantilly cream rosettes on top of the torte in a spoke design.

Push pastry wedge gently but firmly into cream

9 Top with the wedges of pastry, setting them at an angle with one long edge alongside a strip of Chantilly cream.

10 Put a whole strawberry in the gaps between the pastry wedges. Pipe a large swirled rosette of Chantilly cream in the center of the torte. Strip the mint leaves from the sprigs and arrange them decoratively on top of the torte.

🍽 **TO SERVE**
Cut between the pastry wedges. Serve the raspberry coulis separately.

Mint leaves are bright, fresh color contrast

Crisp hazelnut pastry wedges are irresistible with whipped cream and strawberries

VARIATION

ALMOND TORTE WITH PEACHES

Almonds replace the hazelnuts in Hazelnut Torte with Strawberries and the pastry is layered with sliced fresh peaches instead of the berries.

1 Toast 1 ⅔ cups whole blanched almonds in the same way as the hazelnuts, allowing 12-15 minutes. They do not need to be skinned.
2 Prepare the pastry dough as directed, using the almonds, and press out the rounds. Bake 12-15 minutes, then trim and cut one of the rounds into wedges as directed.
3 Immerse 6 medium ripe peaches (total weight about 1½ lb) in a saucepan of boiling water, leave 10 seconds, then transfer to a bowl of cold water. Cut each peach in half, remove the pit, and peel off the skin. Slice the peach halves.
4 Assemble the torte as directed, reserving some peach slices for the top. Pipe 8 spiral rosettes of Chantilly cream and arrange the pastry wedges between them with the reserved peach slices next to them.

FRUIT KNOW-HOW

Home-grown fruit beats all others. Depending on the location and climate, if you have your own trees you can enjoy the fruit of your labors (no pun intended!), at least for a brief season in the year. Small farmers' markets embody this principle and often carry produce that is exceptional because it is locally picked and tree-ripened. They may also offer rarer varieties of fruit than can be found in larger stores and supermarkets.

CHOOSING FRUIT

Modern technology has brought considerable changes to the production of fruit. It is tempting to condemn this, given inferior flavor and the increasing use of chemical sprays. But these changes are counter-balanced by huge benefits: our favorite fruit can be eaten year-round instead of being a seasonal treat, and the most exotic fruit may appear in your local supermarkets.

It is important to know how to choose fruit at the market. The biggest and brightest fruit is not necessarily the best – in fact, probably far from it! Here are some tips on what to look for when buying specific types of fruit.

Apples: firm and bright with an even background color; no bruises (but brown patches, or russeting, do not mean poor quality). *Pears:* firm, but yielding slightly at the stem end, with the stem still attached. *Peaches and nectarines:* firm but not hard, with a yellow or cream-colored background and a distinct seam along the side; no greenish tinge, bruises, or wrinkled or shriveled skin (brown patches signal decay). *Apricots:* should give when pressed; soft velvety skin with no greenish tinge. *Plums:* uniform in color with smooth skin and slightly soft flesh. *Cherries:* plump, shiny, and well-colored with green, not dark or dry, stems. *Lemons and limes:* smooth skin that is not shriveled. *Oranges:* firm with no blemishes. *Grapefruit:* resilient, with no soft patches. (All citrus fruit should feel heavy with juice.) *Green, red, and black grapes:* unblemished and of uniform color, firmly attached to the stem; good aroma. Red and black grapes should not have a greenish tinge. *Strawberries:* uniform color and moist green hull; perfumed aroma. *Raspberries,*

blackberries, boysenberries, and other soft berries: plump with brilliant-to-deep color; no mold or rot. *Blueberries and other firm berries:* plump and shiny, with deep color. (Always buy berries in small containers because those in large containers may be crushed by their own weight.) *Dessert melons, such as honeydew, cantaloupe, Crenshaw, and casaba:* heavy for their size and firm, with no soft spots, cracks, or mold; a heady aroma with no rotting overtones. *Watermelons:* deep green, matt skin; shake small ones because loose seeds indicate ripeness. *Bananas:* fairly soft skin when ripe, possibly with brown spots; no black patches. *Pineapples:* large and heavy with sweet aroma and central leaves that can be pulled out from the plume. *Mangoes:* a sweet smell and taut skin with no soft spots. *Papayas:* small, with deep color. *Kiwi fruit:* should yield slightly, with no soft spots. *Passion fruit:* dry shriveled skin and heavy for its size. *Pomegranates:* large and heavy in your hand, with clean skin. *Persimmons:* bright orange when ripe, with soft yielding pulp. *Star fruit or carambola:* firm, with juicy flesh. *Lychee nuts:* unbroken bumpy skin, pink to brownish in color. *Purple and green figs:* dry with a sweet odor and no blemishes.

FRUIT AND YOUR HEALTH

With health concerns on the rise, many cooks turn to fruit desserts for their high vitamin content and low calories. Several of the recipes in **Fruit Desserts** are naturally healthy, containing little or no butter, eggs, heavy cream, or sugar. Summer Fruit Salad and Mango Sorbet are two delicious examples. And with the simple modifications suggested here, other, richer fruit desserts can be made healthier and less fattening so that you can enjoy a balance between taste and nutrition.

The sugar in every recipe can be reduced according to taste, and polyunsaturated margarine can be substituted for butter (although pastry recipes will suffer in taste and texture). You can omit Chantilly cream accompaniments and decorations: Pear and Red-Currant Compote, Baked Peaches with Amaretti Cookies, and Cherry Strudel lighten up considerably when you leave out the whipped cream on the side. Make fruit tartlets and tarts without the pastry cream, and serve soufflé puddings without the custard sauce – and you're on your way to making desserts that are healthier but just as pleasurable.

If you have a specific health problem, consult your physician and follow his recommended diet.

CLEANING FRUIT

Fruit that is eaten with its skin may be washed gently in cold or warm water but should never be left to soak or it will become soggy. Water also encourages rotting in soft fruit, so avoid washing delicate fruit such as berries unless they are very sandy. Some fruit, such as apples and citrus fruit, may be preserved with an edible wax; this can usually be removed by scrubbing the fruit under running water. Most modern pesticides used on fruit cannot be eliminated by washing; however, peeling fruit will reduce contamination.

PREVENTING DISCOLORATION

When exposed to air, certain tannins and enzymes in fruit such as apples, peaches, and pears react, turning the cut fruit brown. Acid helps prevent this: rub the cut surfaces of the fruit with a halved lemon or lime, or immerse it in water mixed with a little lemon or lime juice (this is called "acidulation"). Always peel or cut these fruit with a stainless steel knife because other metals may encourage discoloration. Fruit that discolors should be prepared as quickly as possible, just before it is needed.

STORING FRUIT

The type of fruit, and how ripe it is when you buy it, determines how long it can be kept. Some fruit, such as apples, pears, and oranges, ripen relatively slowly. Others – grapes and berries, for example – become ripe or overripe within a few days of maturity and cannot be stored for long. Fully ripened fruit should be refrigerated immediately. Discard any overripe or moldy pieces – berries are particularly susceptible to mold. Handle fruit gently because bruising or crushing encourages rot.

If a piece of fruit needs to ripen further at home, keep it at room temperature. It will ripen more quickly if wrapped, so store the fruit in a brown paper bag punctured with holes. If the fruit is extremely hard, the process can be accelerated by adding a very ripe piece of fruit to the bag. Some fruit, such as apples, nectarines, berries, and pears, will rot if left with their skins touching. If ripening them for more than a day, spread them out or wrap them individually in paper.

HOW-TO BOXES

*There are pictures of all preparation steps for each **Fruit Desserts** recipe. Some basic techniques are general to a number of recipes; they are shown in extra detail in these special "how-to" boxes.*

INDEX

ACKNOWLEDGMENTS

Photographer David Murray
Photographer's Assistant Jules Selmes

Chef Eric Treuille
Cookery Consultant Linda Collister
Home Economist Sarah Loman

US Editor Jeanette Mall

Typesetting Rowena Feeny
Text film by Disc to Print (UK) Limited

Production Consultant Lorraine Baird

*Anne Willan would like to thank
her chief editor Cynthia Nims and
associate editor Kate Krader for their
vital help with writing the book and
researching and testing the recipes,
aided by La Varenne's chefs
and trainees.*